Witness Lee

Basic Lessons on Service

Living Stream Ministry
Anaheim, California

First Edition, 4,000 copies. October 1993.

ISBN 0-87083-733-8

Published by

Living Stream Ministry
1853 W. Ball Road, Anaheim, CA 92804 U.S.A.
P. O. Box 2121, Anaheim, CA 92814 U.S.A.

Printed in the United States of America

CONTENTS

PREFACE

These basic lessons on service were given by Brother Witness Lee from February through December 1979 in Anaheim, California. They were given to the elders and co-workers in Southern California for the purpose of training the saints.

HOW TO MEET

Scripture Reading: Matt. 18:20; Acts 2:1; 14:27; 20:7; 1 Cor. 14:19, 23a, 25b, 26; 11:17; Heb. 10:25

OUTLINE

 I. The church being the assembly, the gathering of the called-out ones.
 II. To meet being to worship God and to serve Him.
III. To meet being to minister Christ to others.
 IV. To meet being to build up the church—1 Cor. 14:4b, 26.
 V. How to meet:
   A. Into the Lord's name.
   B. By exercising our spirit—1 Cor. 14:32.
   C. With the experience of Christ.
   D. Ministering Christ.
   E. By prophesying—1 Cor. 14:31.
   F. Without division—1 Cor. 11:17-18.
Focus: To meet is to serve, to minister.

We need to teach people that when we use the term *service* we are not referring to the so-called Sunday morning service in the denominations. Not only has Christianity spoiled the word *service,* but even among us this word has been spoiled to some extent. When we use the word *service,* we may think of our service groups in the church life or the service office. Actually in the New Testament, the Greek word for *service* really means ministry. To minister is to serve people with something. If I serve you without ministering something to you, that is wrong.

In the New Testament, the service, or the ministry, is the stewardship (1 Cor. 9:17; Eph. 3:2; Col. 1:25). A steward is always serving people with something. The stewardesses on the airplane are a good illustration of this. They serve people on the plane with food, with drinks, with blankets, with pillows, or with things to read. They serve you with something, which means that they minister something to you. A waiter in a restaurant is also a good illustration of one who serves people with something. We have to make this point clear to the saints. To serve is not just to come to clean the meeting hall. Service is ministry.

There is only one ministry in the New Testament (2 Cor. 4:1). As long as we minister Christ according to the apostles' teaching (Acts 2:42), the teaching of God's New Testament economy (1 Tim. 1:3-4), we are in the one ministry. The one ministry is the ministry of Christ to people for the producing and the building up of the church, the Body of Christ. When we see this we can realize that the interpretation or the application among Christians today of the word *ministry* is not accurate. We have to come back to the pure meaning of this New Testament word to see a clear vision of the New Testament ministry.

The first thing we have to help the saints with concerning the service is how to meet. I do not think that many Christians would consider that to meet is to serve. Meeting is a ministry. Meeting is a service. Immediately after we are saved, the first service we have to render to God is to meet. If you have not come together with the saints to meet, you have never begun your ministry. The first time you attended the church meeting, that was the beginning of your service. This is because in the meetings we render our worship to God, and this is the service. We worship God and we serve God in our meetings, and in our meetings we offer our praises and our thanks to God.

The crucial thing in the meetings is that we offer Christ to God. At our conversion God gave us His Son as a gift. Immediately after we are saved, we come to worship God in our meetings to render God's gift, Christ, to the Father. This is our offering to God. At our conversion God gave His Son to us as a gift. When we were saved, we became the sons of God. Now we have to serve God, to come to the meetings to offer Christ to God as the unique gift which God the Father has given to us. Our ministry toward God is to minister Christ to God.

According to the type in the Old Testament, the priests ministered to God with offerings. They offered their burnt offerings, meal offerings, and peace offerings to God. These were things ministered to God for His satisfaction. This is the top service. It is a shame that we Christians have missed this kind of understanding. We never considered that to come to the meeting to offer Christ to God is our top service.

In ancient times, all the Israelites came together to worship God three times a year (Deut. 16:16). The first thing they did was to bring all the rich surplus of the produce of the good land and offer this surplus to God for God's satisfaction. That was the top service they rendered to God. That type has to be fulfilled today in the New Testament with us. Our salvation was our Passover. Now that we have received God's salvation with Christ as our Passover, we must offer Christ to God. Offering Christ to God is our service. The more that we stress this, the better. Very few would consider that we meet to serve God and that our service is our ministry. To meet is to serve, to minister.

I. THE CHURCH BEING THE ASSEMBLY, THE GATHERING OF THE CALLED-OUT ONES

As a basis for realizing the importance of the meetings and how to meet, we need to see that in the most basic sense, the church is the assembly, the gathering of the called-out ones. The term *church* in Greek *(ekklesia)* means a kind of called assembly. In ancient times when a city called its people together for a certain purpose, this was always called an *ekklesia,* which was an assembly, a gathering of the called-out ones. The Bible uses the word *ekklesia* to indicate the church because it really corresponds with the meaning of the church. The church is a gathering of God's called-out ones. We have been called out of the world, so we gather together. Whenever we gather together, that gathering is the church.

We need to point out that the Lord Jesus mentioned the church twice in the Gospels—once in Matthew 16:18 referring to the universal church and once in Matthew 18:17 referring to the local church. When the Lord Jesus mentioned the church the second time in Matthew 18:17, it was in the local sense and it indicated the matter of meeting. In verse 20 the Lord said, "Where there are two or three gathered into My name, there am I in their midst." When the Lord Jesus mentioned the matter of the church in a local sense, He pointed out the need of the gathering, the meeting. If we are going to have the Lord's presence, surely we need to meet together.

II. TO MEET BEING TO WORSHIP GOD AND TO SERVE HIM

We have already said that to meet is to worship God and to serve Him. But we need to stress again and again that if a believer does not come to meet with the church, that means he does not worship God and serve Him in an adequate way.

III. TO MEET BEING TO MINISTER CHRIST TO OTHERS

To meet is to minister Christ to others. This point is very crucial. Most Christians have the concept that to come to the meeting is to receive the help. They do not have the sensation, the consideration, or the concept that they need to minister Christ to others. Every believer should have something of Christ. Thus, when we come to the meeting, we come to share Christ with others, to minister Christ to others, either by our prayer, by our testimony, or by our word as a short message. We always have to get ourselves prepared to minister Christ in the meeting. We need to speak more on this point to impress the young ones and the new ones among us. Their wrong concept needs to be corrected.

Even we ourselves have been in the "garlic room" of wrong teachings too long. Because of this, we do not have the sense that it is absolutely a deficiency to come to a meeting without ministering Christ to others. According to the type in the Old Testament, God charged His people not to come to the meeting empty-handed (Deut. 16:16). When you come to the meeting, you must have something to offer. Also, if the priest in the Old Testament did not offer something on the altar, he could never get into the tabernacle. Without anything to offer to God, we can never enter into the tabernacle, so this is a must. If we do not offer something to God, and we try to enter into the presence of God, this is a great deficiency.

IV. TO MEET BEING TO BUILD UP THE CHURCH

We also need to see that to meet is to build up the church (1 Cor. 14:26). First Corinthians 14 says that in a meeting the best thing is to prophesy (v. 31). This is because prophesying builds the church (v. 4b). This tells us clearly that when we come to the meeting, we build up the church. To meet is a service, and this is the building service, the building ministry.

We need to spend a longer time in our sharing to stress this one thing: that every saint has to build up the church. According to Ephesians 4:16, the Body of Christ is built up not only through every joint of the rich supply but also through the operation in measure of each one part. This indicates that every saint must participate in the building up of the Body. This is carried out mainly by coming to the meeting. To meet is the way to build up the church.

Every attendant in the meeting must be a builder to do the building work. But we need to consider our situation today. A number of saints in our meetings would not do anything. They just sit there expecting to receive something. But if all the saints would exercise to build the meeting, surely we would have a strong meeting, a rich meeting, and a high meeting. Suppose not even one saint would function in the meeting, and everyone came to the meeting to sit there dumbly. That would be the lowest meeting, the poorest meeting, a meeting with nothing. The more we open our mouths to speak for the Lord, the more the building work will be done. The more we all exercise to speak Christ in the meetings, the richer, the higher, and the more living the meetings will be. We need to encourage all the saints to minister, to serve, for the building up of the church (1 Cor. 14:3-5).

V. HOW TO MEET

A. Into the Lord's Name

In Matthew 18:20 the Lord said, "For where there are two or three gathered into My name, there am I in their midst." We need to notice that according to the Greek text, it is not to be gathered *in* the Lord's name but *into* His name. Whenever we come to the meeting, we have to come out of our self, out of the world, out of our house, out of our family, out of our job, out of our business, out of our school, and out of everything other than Christ. We have to come into His name. The name of the Lord in the New Testament means His person. When we are gathered into His name, that means we gather into the person of the Lord. We need to come out of many other things and come into the Lord Himself.

B. By Exercising Our Spirit

When we meet, we should always exercise our spirit. This is indicated in 1 Corinthians 14:32, which says, "The spirits of prophets are subject to prophets." In the meetings we do not need to exercise our emotion or mind that much. What is really needed is for us to exercise our spirit.

C. With the Experience of Christ

We should come to the church meetings with the experience of Christ. The New Testament does not say much concerning what we should bring to the meeting, but the New Testament always depends upon the pictures shown in the Old Testament. In the Old Testament, every gathering of God's people ordained by God at the very place chosen by God was for God's people to bring their rich surplus of the good land and offer this surplus to God. God charged them not to come empty-handed. They had to bring the rich surplus of the good land, and the good land typifies Christ. The rich produce of the rich surplus typifies our experience and our enjoyment of Christ. Therefore, we must come to the meeting with the experiences of Christ.

How much content the meeting has and how high the meeting is altogether depend upon how much we have experienced Christ. We must come to the meeting not with the objective, doctrinal Christ but with the subjective, experiential Christ. Many Christians do not have any experience of Christ in their daily walk, so when they come together they do not have anything of Christ to minister to one another. But in the Lord's recovery it should be absolutely different. Day by day we should have some experience of Christ. Then something will be accumulated in our being and we will have something of Christ to minister and impart to others. To get into the name of the Lord, to exercise our spirit, and to offer the Christ whom we have experienced are the basic ways of how we should come together.

D. Ministering Christ

If you come into the person of Christ, exercise your spirit, and have some experience of Christ, whenever you open up your mouth, whether you call a hymn, pray, praise, give a testimony, read a portion of the Word, or speak a short message, it will be the ministering of Christ. Christ will come out of you. This is the ministry, and this is the top service. You will become a steward serving people with Christ. You will become a divine waiter or waitress, waiting on many attendants and serving them with something of Christ.

E. By Prophesying

First Corinthians 14 says that when we come together, we all can prophesy one by one (v. 31) and that prophesying builds up the church (v. 4b). In Exodus 4 Moses told the Lord that he was not an eloquent speaker (v. 10). Then the Lord gave Aaron to Moses to be his co-worker. He said to Moses concerning Aaron, "And thou shalt speak unto him, and put words in his mouth: and I will be with thy mouth, and with his mouth, and will teach you what ye shall do" (v. 15). When Moses would speak to his brother Aaron to put some words into his mouth, God would be with Moses' mouth and with Aaron's mouth. Then the Lord said to Moses, "And he shall be thy spokesman unto the people" (v. 16). Aaron was to be Moses' spokesman. In Exodus 7:1 the Lord said to Moses, "See, I have made thee a god to Pharaoh; and Aaron thy brother shall be thy prophet." That meant that Aaron would speak for Moses. A prophet is a spokesman. The basic meaning of the word *prophesy* is to speak for someone. To prophesy, in the New Testament sense, is to speak for Christ. We need to use 1 Corinthians 14:31 to impress the saints that in the church meetings we all can prophesy one by one.

F. Without Division

In 1 Corinthians 11:17-18 the apostle Paul said, "But I give you this charge and do not praise you, because you come together not for the better but for the worse. For first of all, when you come together in the church, I hear that divisions exist among you; and some part of it I believe." Paul told the Corinthians that they were meeting not for profit but for a loss because they met with divisions. Therefore, we must stay away from any division in the meeting. We should not participate in any divisive meeting.

According to the type in the Old Testament, the children of Israel had to come together to one unique place, and that one unique place kept them all in oneness. Their gathering according to God's way was in oneness and was also a preservation of oneness. The oneness among the children of Israel in ancient times was preserved by their kind of gathering. The children of Israel appeared before the Lord three times a year in the place chosen by God to be gathered together into one. As long as division exists yet we meet, that is not a profit to us but a loss.

The points in this message should be sufficient to give the saints a clear view of how to meet. We need to remember the focus of this message: to meet is to serve, to minister.

THE LORD'S TABLE MEETING

(1)

Scripture Reading: 1 Cor. 11:17-34

OUTLINE

Two categories of meetings:

I. The ministry meetings:

    A. To preach the gospel—Acts 2:6, 14.

    B. To give a report of God's work—Acts 14:26-27.

    C. To read the apostles' writing (the Scripture)—Acts 15:30-31.

II. The church meetings:

    A. The Lord's table meeting:

        1. On the first day of the week (the Lord's Day)—Acts 20:6b-7a; 1 Cor. 16:2.

        2. To partake of the Lord's table—1 Cor. 10:21b.

        3. To eat the Lord's supper—1 Cor. 11:20.

        4. To remember the Lord:

            a. The focus of the Lord's table:

                1) All hymns, praises, thanks, testimonies, and words should be concentrated on the Lord Himself.

                2) All distractions should be avoided.

            b. By breaking the bread to apprehend with appreciation and thanks the Lord's physical body being broken for us—Luke 22:19; 1 Cor. 11:24.

In our first lesson on service, we shared about how to meet. The first meeting we should come to is the Lord's table meeting. Before we fellowship about the Lord's table meeting, we need to see the two categories of meetings in the Bible.

I. THE MINISTRY MEETINGS

First, there are the ministry meetings. The ministry means the work. The meetings for the work are for three basic purposes: preaching the gospel, giving a report of God's work, and reading the apostles' writing (the Scripture).

A. To Preach the Gospel

The work meetings, the ministry meetings, are for preaching the gospel. Acts 2 shows the first preaching of the gospel conducted by Peter at the very beginning of the church life (vv. 6, 14). That was not a meeting of the church, but a meeting for the work, a ministry meeting, to preach the gospel.

B. To Give a Report of God's Work

The ministry meetings are also for giving a report of God's work. After Paul took his first evangelical trip, he came back to Antioch, from where he was sent, and called a meeting to give the saints a report concerning God's work among the Gentiles (Acts 14:26-27). That was not a meeting of the church. It was a meeting of the ministry.

C. To Read the Apostles' Writing (the Scripture)

The ministry meetings are also for reading the apostles' writing (the Scripture). This is shown in Acts 15:30-31. After the conference in Jerusalem, the apostles and elders made a decision to write something. Then some went out to gather the saints together and read this writing to them. This gathering was not a meeting of the church, but a meeting of the ministry. At that time they were listening to the writing of the apostles. Eventually, the apostles' writings became the Scripture. This implies that a ministry meeting may be for the purpose of reading and studying the Scripture.

In the New Testament there are mainly three things

carried out in the ministry meetings: preaching the gospel, giving a report of God's work, and studying and ministering the Word. When we come together to listen to the ministry of the Word, that is not a church meeting but a ministry meeting.

II. THE CHURCH MEETINGS

The second category of meetings is the church meetings, and the first meeting of the church which we need to consider is the Lord's table meeting.

A. The Lord's Table Meeting

1. On the First Day of the Week (the Lord's Day)

Acts 2 tells us that the early believers had the Lord's table, the breaking of bread, every day in their homes (vv. 42, 46). Later in Acts 20:6b-7a, we can see that the saints had a habit of having the Lord's table on the Lord's Day, the first day of the week. Verse 6b says that the apostle Paul and his co-workers stayed in Troas for seven days. Then the next verse says that on the first day of the week they had the Lord's table. This strongly indicates that by that time the Lord's table was conducted mainly on the Lord's Day, the first day of the week, the day of resurrection.

We need to say a little word here about the difference between the Lord's Day and Sunday. *Sunday* is a heathen, idolatrous term adopted by Catholicism and maintained by our tradition. Actually, it is idolatrous to say a day belongs to the sun. The Bible refers to this day as the first day of the week. Revelation 1:10 calls this day "the Lord's Day." We must respect the first day of the week as a memorial of the Lord's resurrection. We should consider this day as a day of the Lord and for the Lord.

Today the whole world takes Sunday not mainly for worship but for pleasures, for sports, and for all kinds of entertainment. This is more evil than idol worship, but this tide has flooded many Christians. Many Christians not only refer to the Lord's Day as *Sunday,* but also consider Sunday as a day of pleasure and entertainment. We, however, should consider the first day of the week as a day for the Lord.

In ancient times, the saints eventually had the Lord's table on the Lord's Day, the first day of every week. This is also proved by 1 Corinthians 16:2. In this verse the apostle Paul told the saints that on the first day of each week, they should offer something of their material possessions to the Lord. This proves that on the first day of each week, the early saints met together. Today the best day for the Christians to meet together is the first day of the week, the Lord's Day. We must make this clear to the saints.

2. To Partake of the Lord's Table

The Lord's table is a feast. First Corinthians 10:21b uses the term *the Lord's table*. We must tell the saints that the table here means the feast. We come to the Lord's table to enjoy a feast.

3. To Eat the Lord's Supper

First Corinthians 11:20 refers to our eating the Lord's supper. This is not a breakfast or a lunch, but a supper, a dinner. When the Lord established the table, He did it in the evening of the Passover, so it was a supper.

Here we must stress that the Lord's table is not only a feast but also a supper. A feast is mainly a kind of enjoyment, and a supper is a kind of restful eating. After a day's work, after a day's labor, people restfully eat their supper. Thus, we come to the Lord's table not only to enjoy it as a feast, but also to take it restfully. After we eat breakfast, we labor, but the Lord's table is a supper for us to rest. No labor is implied here, but rest. Generally speaking, supper does not imply any kind of work, any kind of labor, or any intention to work. Supper indicates that the work is over, and now is the time for rest.

4. To Remember the Lord

Here we must say a strong word to correct a wrong concept. Many Christians think that to have the Lord's table is to remember His death. This is wrong. We are not going to remember the death, but we are going to remember the Lord Himself. The Lord told us to do this in remembrance of Him, not of His death. We remember the Person, the Lord Himself. This is the central point of the Lord's table meeting.

a. The Focus of the Lord's Table

The Lord's table meeting is to remember the Lord, so any hymns, testimonies, or messages that distract people from the Lord, the Person, are not appropriate. In the Lord's table meeting, someone may call a hymn on fighting the battle, or in the midst of the Lord's table, someone may give a testimony of how he was rescued from his suffering. That might be good in another kind of meeting, but it is not fitting at the Lord's table meeting. A brother may come to the Lord's table with a good verse which he enjoyed in his time of morning revival. He might come with that good verse to give people a good teaching concerning repentance and salvation. This is wrong. Such a teaching is not for the Lord's table meeting but for a gospel-preaching meeting. The Lord's table meeting is concentrated on the Person of the Lord, so all the hymns, all the praises, and all the speaking should be concentrated on the Lord Himself. All distractions from the focus of the Lord's table should be avoided.

b. By Breaking the Bread to Apprehend with Appreciation and Thanks the Lord's Physical Body Being Broken for Us

We remember the Lord by breaking the bread, by eating the bread, and by drinking the cup. In this lesson we want to talk only about breaking the bread. We remember the Lord not by thinking about, memorizing, or reckoning what the Lord did, but by breaking the bread. We break the bread to apprehend with appreciation and thanks the Lord's physical body being broken for us (Luke 22:19; 1 Cor. 11:24). Many of us do not care for the meaning of breaking the bread. We break the bread in the meeting to signify that the Lord's physical body was broken on the cross for us and for our sins.

In the next lesson we will cover more concerning our remembrance of the Lord at the Lord's table. The next crucial point we will see is our eating of the bread to enjoy the Lord as our life supply, to testify that we live by the Lord, and to have fellowship in Christ's mystical Body. Then we will fellowship concerning displaying the Lord's death, expressing our desire of the Lord's coming back, and worshipping the Father.

THE LORD'S TABLE MEETING

(2)

Scripture Reading: 1 Cor. 10:16-17; 11:24-34; Matt. 26:27-30

OUTLINE

4. To remember the Lord:
    c. By eating the bread:
        1) To enjoy the Lord as our life supply—John 6:35a.
        2) To testify that we live by the Lord—John 6:57b.
        3) To have fellowship in Christ's mystical Body—1 Cor. 10:16b-17.
    d. By drinking the cup—1 Cor. 11:25:
        1) To review the redemption of the new covenant—Matt. 26:27-28.
        2) To receive God's blessing.
        3) To have fellowship in the blood of Christ—1 Cor. 10:16a.
5. To display the Lord's death—1 Cor. 11:26.
6. To express our desire of the Lord's coming back—1 Cor. 11:26b; Matt. 26:29.
7. To worship the Father—Matt. 26:30.
8. Warning:
    a. Proving ourselves and discerning the Body—1 Cor. 11:28-29.
    b. Not eating the bread and drinking the cup unworthily—1 Cor. 11:27.
    c. For the worse, if meeting with divisions—1 Cor. 11:17-18.

        d. The Lord's chastening—1 Cor. 11:30-34.

Focus: The real remembrance of the Lord is to receive and enjoy Him as our life supply by eating and drinking Him and by sharing Him one with another in the fellowship of His Body.

In this lesson we want to continue our fellowship on the Lord's table meeting. In the previous lesson, we saw that the focus of the Lord's table is the Lord Himself. We also saw that we remember the Lord by breaking the bread to apprehend with appreciation and thanks the Lord's physical body being broken for us. Now we want to consider more points concerning our remembrance of the Lord.

c. By Eating the Bread

1) To Enjoy the Lord as Our Life Supply

In John 6:35a the Lord told us that He is the bread of life, so to eat the bread is to enjoy the Lord as our life supply. Breaking the bread does not imply any enjoyment, but eating the bread surely does.

2) To Testify That We Live by the Lord

We also eat the bread to testify that we live by the Lord. In John 6:57b the Lord said, "He who eats Me, he also shall live because of Me." By eating the bread we indicate that we enjoy the Lord and we testify that this is our way to live. This is the real remembrance of the Lord.

3) To Have Fellowship in Christ's Mystical Body

The next crucial point concerning our remembrance of the Lord is our eating the bread to enjoy the fellowship in Christ's mystical Body. The breaking of the bread mainly implies the Lord's physical body broken for us on the cross. Eating the bread, which is to take in the bread, mainly implies the fellowship in the mystical Body of Christ (1 Cor. 10:16b-17). The same bread, the same loaf on the table, signifies the physical body of Christ and the mystical Body of Christ. The Lord's physical body was broken on the cross for our redemption, and the Lord's mystical Body, the Body of Christ, is for our fellowship. Regarding the Lord's physical body, we break the bread, and regarding His mystical Body, we eat the bread. Eating together means communion, fellowship. A part of the same bread gets into you, a part gets into me, and a part gets into each one of us. This is the oneness in the Body in the fellowship of the Body.

We need to spend time on this point, especially for the sake of the new ones and young ones among us. First, the bread on the table signifies the Lord Jesus' physical body He gave for us on the cross. This is the bread which we break. Second, the bread also signifies the Lord's mystical Body, which is composed of all the saved believers. When the Lord Jesus was on this earth, He was a grain of wheat (John 12:24). But today He is no longer merely a single grain of wheat. He is the bread composed of the many grains, including Himself. Thus, to eat the bread implies that we are participating in the mystical Body of Christ, comprising all the saints, that is, we are fellowshipping with all the saints universally from ancient times until today. We need to see that the remembrance of the Lord at His table implies His redemption, His Body, and His entire New Testament economy.

d. By Drinking the Cup

We also remember the Lord by drinking the cup (1 Cor. 11:25).

1) To Review the Redemption of the New Covenant

Our drinking the cup is to review the redemption of the new covenant. For this point it would be good to read Matthew 26:27-28: "And He took a cup and gave thanks, and He gave it to them, saying, Drink of it, all of you, for this is My blood of the covenant, which is being poured out for many for the forgiveness of sins."

2) To Receive God's Blessing

To eat the bread is to receive life; to drink the cup is to receive blessing. In the Bible, the bread is called the bread of life (John 6:35a) and the cup is called the cup of blessing (1 Cor. 10:16a). Thus, to eat the bread means to receive the life supply and to drink the cup means to receive the blessing.

The cup indicates a portion—either a portion of wrath or a portion of blessing. If we are condemned under God's judgment, the cup is a portion of wrath to us (Rev. 14:10). If we are forgiven and redeemed, the cup is a portion of blessing to us. The Bible does not say that we drink the blood but that we drink the cup. This means that the redeeming blood of the Lord Jesus becomes our cup, our portion.

When we drink the cup, we not only review the redemption of the new covenant but also receive God's blessing. This blessing is God Himself. Adam's fall caused man to lose God, but Christ's redemption brings God back to man. The losing of God in man's fall was the greatest loss. Now our gaining God back in Christ's redemption is the unique blessing. The cup as a portion is God Himself as the unique blessing to us.

Through this fellowship we can see how much the Lord's table implies. To remember the Lord is not merely to remember how He was God and how He became a man. To remember the Lord is to break the bread, to eat the bread, and to drink the cup in the reality of all their deep significances.

3) To Have Fellowship in the Blood of Christ

Drinking the cup also indicates that we have fellowship in the blood of Christ (1 Cor. 10:16a). We have a joint and mutual participation in the drinking of the one cup. Both eating and drinking indicate oneness and fellowship, communion. This is why we have only one loaf, not many loaves, and only one cup, not many cups, at the table. One loaf and one cup indicate the oneness and the fellowship, the communion. This communion, this fellowship, is in both the mystical Body of Christ and in the redeeming blood of Christ. Because we all are redeemed by this one blood, we have the one communion, and through this we receive the unique blessing.

5. To Display the Lord's Death

At the Lord's table, we do not remember the Lord's death, but we declare, proclaim, display, the Lord's death. First Corinthians 11:26 says, "For as often as you eat this bread and drink the cup, you declare the Lord's death until He comes." Here we have the bread signifying the Lord's body, and we have the cup signifying the Lord's blood. On the Lord's table, His death is displayed, because the cup is separate from the bread, that is, the blood is separate from the body. We eat the bread and we drink the cup to display the Lord's death, because whenever the blood is separate from the body, that is death. Whenever we eat the bread and drink the cup, we do not remember the Lord's death but we display His death to the whole universe, especially to the principalities and powers in the heavenlies.

6. To Express Our Desire of the Lord's Coming Back

We also remember the Lord at His table to express our desire of His coming back. First Corinthians 11:26b says that we display the Lord's death until He comes. While we display the Lord's death, we express our desire of the Lord's second coming. In Matthew 26:29 the Lord said, "I shall by no means drink of this product of the vine from now on until that day when I drink it new with you in the kingdom of My Father." This is the manifestation of the kingdom of the heavens, in which the Lord will drink with us after His coming back. When we remember the Lord and display His death, we express our desire that the Lord will come back soon.

7. To Worship the Father

After all of this, the Lord will lead us to worship the Father. This is based upon Matthew 26:30, which says that after the Lord finished His supper with His disciples, He and the disciples sang a hymn. That hymn was sung by the Lord with His disciples to the Father. In the Lord's table, the Lord takes the lead to praise the Father, to worship the Father. At the end of the Lord's table meeting, we need to worship the Father with the Lord. We must follow the firstborn Son to worship the Father as His brothers. The Lord as the firstborn Son takes the lead to worship the Father (Heb. 2:12), and we as His many brothers follow Him.

Hymn #52 (Hymns) is a very good hymn on the worship of the Father. Stanzas 2 and 3 say:

2 How deep the holy joy that fills that scene,
    Where love is known!
Thy love, our God and Father, now is seen,
    In Him alone;
As, in the holy calm of Thine own rest,
He leads the praise of those Thy love has blessed.

3 He leads the praise! How precious to Thine ear
    The song He sings!
How precious, too, to Thee—how near, how dear
    Are those He brings
To share His place: 'twas thus that Thou didst plan;
Thou lovedst Him before the world began.

This hymn is simple and short, yet high in its thought and full of light. It would be good to ask the saints to read these stanzas so that they can be impressed with the significance of worshipping the Father.

8. Warning

Related to our partaking of the Lord's table, there is also a warning in the Scriptures.

a. Proving Ourselves and Discerning the Body

We have to prove ourselves and discern the Body at the Lord's table (1 Cor. 11:28-29). We have to discern whether the bread on the table signifies the unique Body of Christ or a sect, a division, a denomination. This is why we can take the Lord's table only in the local churches. We cannot partake of the so-called communion in other places because that bread on the table does not signify the Body but a division. Whenever we go to a place to attend the Lord's table, we must prove to ourselves that the bread on the table really signifies the Lord's Body, without any division.

b. Not Eating the Bread and Drinking the Cup Unworthily

In 1 Corinthians 11:27 we are warned not to eat the bread and drink the cup in an unworthy manner. If you are in division and you still eat the bread and drink the cup, that

means you are eating and drinking unworthily. According to
1 Corinthians 11, there was a kind of looseness and lightness
among the saints in Corinth. Everyone behaved according to
his own likes or dislikes. The divisions and parties among
them spoiled the Lord's table (vv. 17-22). This shows that if
we take the Lord's table with a divisive spirit, we are
partaking of it in an unworthy manner. We should not partake
of the Lord's table in a light, loose, or careless way.

c. For the Worse, If Meeting with Divisions

First Corinthians 11:17-18 shows that if we take the Lord's
table with divisions, our coming together is not for the better
but for the worse. For the better means for a profit. For the
worse means for a loss. It is not a profit but a loss if we
take the Lord's table in division.

d. The Lord's Chastening

If we take the Lord's table in an unworthy manner, the
Lord will come in to chasten us (1 Cor. 11:30-34). The Lord's
judgment upon those in Corinth who participated unworthily
in the Lord's table was to cause them to become weak
physically. Since they would not repent of their offense, they
were further disciplined and became sick. Because they would
still not repent, the Lord judged them by death. This is the
Lord's chastening, the Lord's judgment upon the believers in
this age who would willfully continue to partake of His table
in an unworthy manner. Sometimes when a believer is sick,
he may need to call for the elders of the church and ask them
to pray over him (James 5:14). That means he needs to get
himself reconciled with the Body.

We all need to be trained to partake of the Lord's table
in a proper way. In the past we had the Lord's table in an
untrained way. But now we are going to have the Lord's table
in a civilized way, in a cultured way, in a trained way. In the
past we ate wildly, without "table manners." Now we are
training the saints to have table manners. The table manners
at the Lord's table are not formal things. To have proper table
manners at His table means that we exercise our spirit and
release our praise to Him in the right way. This is a great

thing. The Lord's table is the best meeting, but it is the most difficult meeting for us to have. No other meeting exposes where we are as much as the Lord's table meeting does.

We need to remember the focus of our fellowship in this message. The focus is that the real remembrance of the Lord is to receive and enjoy Him as our life supply by eating and drinking Him and by sharing Him one with another in the fellowship of His Body.

LESSON FOUR

THE PRACTICE OF
THE LORD'S TABLE MEETING

(1)

Scripture Reading: 1 Cor. 11:23-25

OUTLINE

I. Remembering the Lord—1 Cor. 11:24-25:
  A. By praising instead of by praying:
     1. Not to ask the Lord to do things for us.
     2. But to bless the Lord with well-speaking concerning His person and work—Rev. 5:13.
  B. Addressing praise to the Lord Jesus Christ, the Son of God:
     1. Realizing the economy of the Divine Trinity—Matt. 28:19b; 2 Cor. 13:14.
     2. Learning to differentiate the Lord's names from the Father's names (see hymns 65-80, *Hymns*).
  C. Calling hymns:
     1. Learning to know the hymns:
        a. In their categories.
        b. In their contents.
        c. In their focus.
        d. In their sensation and taste.
     2. Learning to apply the hymns at the appropriate time:
        a. To start a section of the meeting.
        b. To strengthen and enrich the started section.
        c. To prolong and uplift the same section.
        d. To follow the atmosphere of the meeting.
  D. Distributing the bread and the cup:

1. Neither too early nor too late.
2. When the remembrance of the Lord reaches the high tide.
3. Better with some thanks given to the Lord— Luke 22:19a.

Focus: The proper remembrance of the Lord depends upon our proper practice.

In this lesson we want to begin to fellowship about the practice of the Lord's table meeting. We do not want to explain what it means to remember the Lord but to say something about the practice of remembering the Lord.

I. REMEMBERING THE LORD

A. By Praising instead of by Praying

To remember the Lord (1 Cor. 11:24-25) we have to praise Him, not pray to Him. Remembering the Lord at His table is by praising instead of by praying.

1. Not to Ask the Lord to Do Things for Us

We do not come to the Lord's table meeting to ask the Lord to do things for us.

2. But to Bless the Lord with Well-speaking concerning His Person and Work

At the Lord's table meeting, we should bless the Lord with well-speaking concerning His person and work. Well-speaking means praising by speaking the good things. Here we need to use Revelation 5:13 as a reference: "And every creature which is in heaven and on the earth and under the earth and on the sea and all things in them, I heard saying, To Him who sits upon the throne and to the Lamb be the blessing and the honor and the glory and the might forever and ever."

We have to impress the saints that it is altogether not fitting to pray to the Lord at the Lord's table when we are remembering Him. Instead, we have to praise Him, to bless Him, to speak well about Him concerning His person. It would be helpful to itemize some of the main points concerning His person, such as His divinity, His humanity, and His statuses as the Son of God, the Son of Man, the Savior, the Redeemer, the Sanctifier, the life-giving Spirit, the Lord, etc. We have to try the best to point out the different items of the Lord's person so that the saints can be helped in their praising. Then we also have to point out the various aspects of the Lord's work, such as His redemptive work, His saving work, His sanctifying work, His transforming work, etc. We have to bless the Lord in such a way as to praise Him, to speak well about Him.

B. Addressing Praise to the Lord Jesus Christ, the Son of God

In the section of remembering the Lord, all our praises should be addressed directly to the Lord Jesus Christ, the Son of God.

1. Realizing the Economy of the Divine Trinity

To address our praises directly to the Lord Jesus, the Son of God, we need to realize the economy of the Divine Trinity. Matthew 28:19b says that we are baptized into the name of the Father, of the Son, and of the Spirit. Second Corinthians 13:14 refers to the love of God, the grace of Christ, and the fellowship of the Spirit. These verses reveal the economy of the Divine Trinity to dispense Himself into His chosen and redeemed people.

2. Learning to Differentiate the Lord's Names from the Father's Names

We need to learn to differentiate the Lord's names from the Father's names. In our personal time it would be good to read *Hymns,* #65 through #80, concerning the names of the Lord. In order to address or praise the Lord Himself directly, we need to know His names.

C. Calling Hymns

1. Learning to Know the Hymns

In order to call the appropriate hymns in the table meeting, we need to learn to know the hymns first in their categories. The table of contents in our hymnal can help us with this, since it categorizes all of the hymns. Then we need to read and even to study the contents of the hymns. We also need to find out the central thought, the focus, of each hymn. Finally, we need to know the hymns in their sensation and taste. Each hymn has its own sensation, so it has its own taste. When you know the hymns in these four aspects—in their categories, contents, focus, and sensation and taste—you know the hymns thoroughly.

2. Learning to Apply the Hymns at the Appropriate Time

We also need to learn how to apply the hymns at the appropriate time. Certain hymns are good for certain times in the meeting, so we have to know the hymns first and then apply them at the proper time.

Certain hymns are very good to start a section of the meeting. After a section of the meeting has been started, we may need another hymn to strengthen and enrich the started section. To strengthen and enrich what has been started is not so easy. Teamwork is involved here. One person starts, and all the others have to continue to strengthen and to enrich what has been started. Also a hymn may be needed to prolong and uplift the same section. Here there is the need of skill. Something has been started and strengthened and enriched, but within a short time it may disappear. This is why we have to prolong it and uplift it.

Furthermore, to apply the hymns at the appropriate time, we need to follow the atmosphere of the meeting. If the atmosphere of the meeting is solemn, a hymn of joy, a rejoicing hymn, does not fit the atmosphere. Thus, calling a proper hymn at a proper time depends upon how much we can sense the atmosphere of the meeting.

D. Distributing the Bread and the Cup

1. Neither Too Early nor Too Late

The proper distributing of the bread and the cup also requires our learning. We should distribute the bread and the cup neither too early nor too late. This is somewhat like serving a meal. One does not serve the main course at the very beginning of the meal nor after the dessert has been finished. This is either too early or too late.

2. When the Remembrance of the Lord
Reaches the High Tide

We need to distribute the bread and the cup when the remembrance of the Lord reaches the high tide. This means that the atmosphere of our remembering the Lord has reached the highest point.

3. Better with Some Thanks Given to the Lord

Furthermore, it is better to distribute the bread and the cup with some thanks given to the Lord. We receive the bread and the wine mostly in a silent way. It is better to receive the bread that comes from the Lord and give Him some thanks. Luke 22:19a says that the Lord took the bread and gave thanks.

The focus of this message is expressed in the following statement: the proper remembrance of the Lord depends upon our proper practice.

THE PRACTICE OF
THE LORD'S TABLE MEETING

(2)

Scripture Reading: Matt. 26:30; Heb. 2:12; Eph. 2:18; John 4:23-24

OUTLINE

II. Worshipping the Father:
  A. After eating the bread and drinking the cup—Matt. 26:26-30.
  B. By praising—Matt. 26:30:
    1. Christ, the Firstborn of God, taking the lead among His brothers—Heb. 2:12.
    2. We, the many sons of God, following Christ in praising the Father.
  C. Addressing praise to the Father:
    1. Through the Son.
    2. In the Spirit—Eph. 2:18.
  D. Calling hymns:
    1. According to the Father's being.
    2. According to the Father's attributes.
  E. By presenting Christ to God the Father:
    1. As the peace offering—Lev. 3.
    2. Enjoying Him before God the Father—Lev. 7:14-21, 28-34:
      a. As life supply—vv. 14-16.
      b. As love in resurrection—vv. 29-31.
      c. As power in ascension—vv. 32-34.
      d. In cleanness—vv. 17-21.

Focus: The worshipping of the Father should be with the Son and in the Spirit (John 4:23-24).

In this lesson we want to see something further concerning the practice of the Lord's table meeting. Matthew 26:30 says that after the breaking of the bread and the drinking of the cup, the Lord and the disciples sang a hymn. Then they went out to the Mount of Olives. Hebrews 2:12 is a strong verse telling us that after Christ's resurrection He declared the Father's name to the disciples and praised the Father in the midst of the church. Then Ephesians 2:18 says that through Christ (who died on the cross and who created the one new man of two peoples) and in the Spirit we come to the Father. This is a brief definition of the dispensing of the Triune God. John 4:23-24 says that the Father today seeks after those who will worship Him in their human spirit and in truthfulness. We worship the Father in our spirit indwelt by the Holy Spirit and in Christ the Son as our reality who becomes our genuineness and sincerity for the true worship of God. We need to impress the saints with the truths revealed in these portions of Scripture.

In the previous lesson, we shared concerning the practice of remembering the Lord at His table. Now we want to speak concerning worshipping the Father.

II. WORSHIPPING THE FATHER

A. After Eating the Bread and Drinking the Cup

Matthew 26:26-30 shows that we should worship the Father after eating the bread and drinking the cup. Verses 26-29 show us that the bread was broken and eaten and that the cup was drunk. Then in verse 30 there is the singing of a hymn to the Father, showing that the worship to the Father must be after eating the bread and drinking the cup.

B. By Praising

We worship the Father by praising. This is also based upon Matthew 26:30. This is a unique verse telling us that a hymn was sung. That means to praise. According to the Greek text, we may say that they "hymned a praise" to the Father. To worship the Father at the Lord's table, we have to sing hymns of praise to Him.

1. Christ, the Firstborn of God,
Taking the Lead among His Brothers

Christ, the Firstborn of God, takes the lead among His brothers to sing hymns of praise to the Father. Hebrews 2:12 says, "I will declare Your name to My brothers; in the midst of the church I will sing hymns of praise to You." The literal meaning according to the Greek is "I will hymn You." Matthew 26:30 and Hebrews 2:12 show us the worship of the Father at the Lord's table. In what kind of meeting can Christ sing hymns of praise to the Father in the midst of His brothers? Matthew 26:30 gives us the answer. Matthew 26:30 is a precious verse showing us that it was after the breaking of the bread and the drinking of the cup that Christ took the lead to sing hymns of praise to the Father among the disciples.

2. We, the Many Sons of God,
Following Christ in Praising the Father

We, the many sons of God, follow Christ in praising the Father. In Matthew 26:30 it was not only Christ but also His disciples singing a hymn of praise with Him. So He took the lead and the disciples followed Him. Today it should be the same. Christ, the Firstborn, takes the lead, and we, the many sons, follow Him to praise the Father.

C. Addressing Praise to the Father

Our addressing praise to the Father is through the Son and in the Spirit. In our remembrance of the Lord, we address all the praises to the Lord. Then when we turn to worship the Father, we have to address all our praises to Him. Ephesians 2:18 says, "For through Him we both have access in one Spirit unto the Father." Through the Son, as the One who died on the cross to abolish all the ordinances and to create the one new man of two peoples (v. 15), and in the Spirit we have access unto the Father.

Ephesians 1 reveals the Father choosing and predestinating us, the Son redeeming us, and the Spirit sealing us. Then 2:18 says that through the Son and in the Spirit, we approach the Father. In chapter three Paul said that he bowed his knees to the Father that He might strengthen us through His Spirit that Christ might make His home in our hearts (vv. 14-17). In chapter four there are three groups: one Body, one Spirit, and one hope; one Lord, one faith, and one baptism; and one God and Father of all, who is over all, through all, and in us all (vv. 4-6). These portions from Ephesians show us the divine economy of the Divine Trinity.

In our sharing it is helpful to link Ephesians 2:18 with Luke 15. Luke 15 reveals that the Son came as the Shepherd to seek after the lost sheep (vv. 1-7), that the Spirit as the woman enlightens the house and eventually finds the lost coin (vv. 8-10), and that the Father receives the returned son (vv. 11-32). This shows the divine economy of the Divine Trinity with the redeeming Son, the sanctifying Spirit, and the receiving Father. Through the Son and in the Spirit, we have access unto the Father. The Lord told three parables in Luke 15 to unveil the saving love of the Triune God toward sinners. The lost sheep, the lost coin, and the lost son are one lost person in three aspects. Luke 15 shows that we cannot be sought for and found and brought to the Father directly. We can come to the Father only through Christ and in the Spirit.

D. Calling Hymns

Now we need to consider our calling of hymns in the section of worshipping the Father at the Lord's table. We need to call hymns according to the Father's being. The Father's name was not revealed until the Lord Jesus came. He came to reveal the name of the Father (John 17:6, 26), the person of the Father. Thus, we have to call hymns according to the Father's person, the Father's being.

We also have to call hymns according to the Father's attributes, such as His love, His kindness, and His glory. In the table of contents of our hymnal under the section entitled "Worship of the Father," we have a number of hymns categorized according to the Father's attributes. These attributes include His faithfulness, His greatness, His wisdom, His mercy, and His love.

We praise the Son according to His person and work, but there is no work with regard to the Father. We should praise the Father according to His being and attributes. We have to differentiate and discern the hymns according to these two categories: the Father's being, what the Father is, and the Father's attributes.

E. By Presenting Christ to God the Father

1. As the Peace Offering

In our worship of the Father, we need to present Christ to Him as the peace offering (Lev. 3). This section is very crucial. To share this with the saints, we need to be clear about the type of the peace offering in the book of Leviticus.

2. Enjoying Him before God the Father

At the Lord's table meeting, we enjoy Christ before God the Father (Lev. 7:14-21, 28-34).

a. As Life Supply

First, we enjoy Christ as our life supply (vv. 14-16). In offering the peace offering, some bread and flesh of the offering was assigned to the priests for their food. That signifies the life supply.

b. As Love in Resurrection

The breast of the offering was assigned to the priests as a wave offering. The breast signifies love and the offering being waved signifies resurrection, so this typifies Christ as love in resurrection to be our life supply (vv. 29-31).

c. As Power in Ascension

The right thigh was assigned to the priest as a heave offering. The right thigh is the strength for movement, signifying Christ as power in ascension (vv. 32-34). At the Lord's table meeting, we enjoy Christ before God the Father as power in ascension.

Thus, we see three kinds of supply with the peace offering: one is the bread and the flesh of the offering, the other is the breast, and the third one is the thigh. One signifies the life supply; the other, love in resurrection; and the other, power in ascension. When Christ ascended to the third heavens, He poured out the Spirit of power. The Spirit of life was given on the day of resurrection, but the Spirit of power was poured out after His ascension. Love is a matter of life, so it is in resurrection, and power is in ascension.

d. In Cleanness

The peace offering in Leviticus had to be presented to God in cleanness (vv. 17-21). This signifies that we enjoy the life supply, love in resurrection, and power in ascension in cleanness. We must be clean. If someone ate the peace offering when he was unclean, he would be cut off from the people. This means that if we are not in cleanness at the Lord's table to present Christ to God the Father, we will be cut off. To be cut off means to lose the fellowship of God's people.

We need to spend some time on this point concerning presenting Christ to God the Father as the peace offering. The peace offering is a wonderful type of Christ being offered to God. We need to see that this peace offering had an enjoyment of three aspects. First, the peace offering was God's food, so it was for the enjoyment of God. Second, the peace offering was also for the enjoyment of the offering priest, the one who presented the offering. Third, the congregation enjoyed their portion of the peace offering under the condition of cleanness. This is all fulfilled in the Lord's table meeting.

In the Lord's table meeting, after the breaking of the bread and the drinking of the cup, on the one hand, Christ takes the lead to sing hymns of praise to God the Father and we follow Him to do this. On the other hand, at the same time, we offer Him as the peace offering to God the Father for God's satisfaction and we enjoy Him as our life supply, as love in resurrection, and as power in ascension. Furthermore, we enjoy Him with one another in cleanness. This is the fulfillment of the presentation of the peace offering in the reality of the New Testament.

Actually, the section in the Lord's table of worshipping the Father is a section to praise the Father and enjoy His

Son with Him. Much of the time our worship to the Father at the Lord's table meeting is inadequate. We need to practice presenting Christ as the peace offering to enjoy Him as our life supply, as our love in resurrection, and as our power in ascension with one another in cleanness.

The focus of this lesson can be expressed in the following statement: the worshipping of the Father should be with the Son and in the Spirit (John 4:23-24). We worship the Father with the Son as the reality and in the Spirit who dwells within our spirit. John 4:23-24 can be fulfilled in our worship to the Father at the Lord's table meeting.

We need to consider the context of John 4:23-24 so that we can understand these verses properly. In verse 20 the Samaritan woman talked with the Lord, saying, "Our fathers worshipped in this mountain, yet you say that in Jerusalem is the place where men must worship." This refers back to Deuteronomy 12, where God ordained that His people worship Him in the unique place chosen by God and with the rich produce of the good land so that they would not be empty-handed when they appeared before God. All of the Israelites had to come to the unique place with the rich produce, the rich offerings, of the good land.

The Lord Jesus indicated to the Samaritan woman that this worship was for the Old Testament age. Then He said, "An hour is coming, and it is now…" (v. 23). In other words, the Lord was saying, "Now the time has come." This means that the age had changed. Now in this new age God the Father is seeking after a kind of worship that is in spirit and in reality.

Here the spirit is our human spirit, and today our human spirit is the unique place where God's dwelling place is. This is based upon Ephesians 2:22, which says that God's habitation today is in our spirit. Since our spirit is the place where God's habitation is, our spirit is today's Jerusalem. We all need to worship God here. This is the unique place. If all Christians would worship God in their spirit, there would be no divisions. Our spirit is the uniting place, the unique center of God's worship, typified by Jerusalem.

We also need to worship God in truthfulness. Truthfulness

denotes the divine reality becoming man's genuineness and sincerity (which are the opposite of the hypocrisy of the immoral Samaritan worshipper) for the true worship of God. The divine reality is Christ as the reality of all the offerings of the Old Testament. Christ is the reality of the rich produce of the good land for our offering.

In order to understand John 4:23-24 properly we have to look at the type in Deuteronomy. In Deuteronomy we see the unique place with all the offerings. Now the Lord says that the unique place is our spirit, and the produce we offer today is not the produce of Canaan but all the riches of Christ. Thus, the unique place is our spirit and the reality is Christ Himself with all His riches. When we partake of Christ as our reality, He becomes the reality within us. This reality within us then becomes our genuineness and sincerity in which we worship God the Father with the worship that He seeks. When we follow the Lord to worship the Father at the Lord's table meeting, we worship the Father with Christ as the rich offerings in the spirit, that is, in our spirit mingled with the Holy Spirit. This is the real worship to God the Father according to His economy.

THE LORD'S TABLE MEETING REPLACING THE FEAST OF THE PASSOVER

The Lord's table meeting is a replacement of the Feast of the Passover. Actually, when the Lord set up His table, He and His disciples were attending the Passover feast. According to the custom of the Jewish Passover, they surely partook of the bread and the wine. Thus, the table meeting set up by the Lord was somewhat transitory. The Lord and the disciples first ate the passover (Matt. 26:20-25; Luke 22:14-18). Then the Lord established His table with the bread and the cup (Matt. 26:26-28; Luke 22:19-20; 1 Cor. 11:23-26) to replace the Feast of the Passover because He was going to fulfill the type and be the real Passover to us (1 Cor. 5:7). Luke 22 shows us that there were two kinds of eating and drinking. One was a part of the Passover (vv. 15-18). The other was a part of the Lord's table (vv. 19-20). Today we are at the Lord's table without any kind of transitory element.

PRAISING THE LORD WITH THE HYMNS

At the Lord's table we should not pray by asking the Lord to do things for us, but we surely need to praise. To praise requires much exercise of the spirit. We need to learn how to praise the Lord after we sing a hymn. We may merely shout, declare, and quote things from the hymnal in a mechanical way. But if the saints are richer and stronger, they will not need to merely quote the hymnal. They will praise the Lord with the thought of the hymn, recomposing some of the terms and phrases. We need to learn how to digest a hymn in our praise. This kind of digestion of a hymn is more living and informal.

In the Lord's table meeting, there needs to be more praise. Instead of praising, the saints may merely read from the hymnal. They must learn to go beyond merely reading a hymn to digesting a hymn. Instead of merely reading, "Oh, what a joy! Oh, what a rest!" (*Hymns,* #499), we can say, "O Lord, in Your life we enjoy the rest. What a rest we enjoy!" We can digest the terms in a hymn and make them a living praise to the Lord.

THE LORD'S TABLE IN ANCIENT TIMES

In the ancient times the believers had a custom of coming together for supper, the main meal of the day, with the rich bringing more and better food for the mutual enjoyment and the poor, less food (1 Cor. 11:21-22). This was called a love feast (2 Pet. 2:13; Jude 12), and it came from the background of the Passover feast (Luke 22:13-20). At the end of their love feast they ate the Lord's supper with the bread and the cup to remember the Lord (1 Cor. 11:23-25). This is the best way to have the Lord's table.

THE CRUCIAL POINT IN OUR SERVICE

We need to be deeply impressed that the crucial point in our service to the Lord is life. Life is the Spirit, and the Spirit is the reality of the living Christ. If we help the saints get on the track of life, all the details of our practice will be spontaneously regulated by life. We need some regulation and regulation helps. But we need to be careful. We are not for a certain regulated situation. A situation that is fully regulated can become like Forest Lawn Cemetery, a situation of death. Brother Nee took the lead to practice the truth with life. We must make it clear to the saints that we are not for the regulations but for life. If the saints grow in life adequately, spontaneously they will be regulated.

THE PRACTICE OF
THE LORD'S TABLE MEETING

(3)

Scripture Reading: John 4:23-24, 14; 1:12; 3:5, 6b; 14:23; 17:26a; Heb. 2:12

OUTLINE

III. The worship in the dispensing of God:
  A. To worship the Father—John 4:23:
    1. By becoming the Father's children—John 1:12; 1 John 3:1a.
    2. By knowing the Father's name—John 17:26a; Heb. 2:12a.
    3. By enjoying the Father's presence—John 14:23.
  B. In the Son as the reality—John 4:23-24:
    1. By experiencing the Son as the good land—Deut. 8:7.
    2. By enjoying the riches of the Son as the rich produce of the good land—Deut. 8:8-10.
    3. By presenting the Son to the Father as the peace offering—Lev. 3:1, 6, 12; 7:11-13.
  C. In our spirit mingled with the Spirit of God—John 4:23-24:
    1. By being born of the Spirit of God in our spirit—John 3:5, 6b.
    2. By being baptized into one Body in the Spirit of God—1 Cor. 12:13a.
    3. By drinking of the Spirit of God—1 Cor. 12:13b; John 4:14.

    4. By being in the unique place of worship where God's habitation is—Deut. 12:5; Eph. 2:22.

D. In the dispensing of the Triune God:

    1. Having been baptized into the Father, the Son, and the Holy Spirit—Matt. 28:19b.

    2. Enjoying the Father's love, the Son's grace, and the Spirit's fellowship—2 Cor. 13:14.

Focus: The worship in the dispensing of the Triune God is the worship to the Father by His many sons with His firstborn Son as the offerings and in His Spirit who mingles Himself with our spirit as the unique place for our worship.

In this lesson we want to continue our fellowship on the practice of the Lord's table meeting. In the previous lessons, we fellowshipped about the practice of remembering the Lord and worshipping the Father. Now we want to see something concerning the worship we need to offer to the Father in the Son as the reality and in our spirit mingled with the Spirit of God. This is a worship in the dispensing of God.

Paul's writings are filled with the concept of the divine dispensing of the Father, the Son, and the Spirit. The Father, the Son, and the Spirit are not referred to by Paul in a doctrinal way but in an experiential way. Ephesians 2:18 reveals that we have access to the Father through the Son and in the Spirit. Ephesians 3 says that the Father strengthens us through His Spirit into the inner man so that Christ, the Son, can make His home in our hearts (vv. 14-17). To praise the Father through the Son and in the Spirit is in the dispensing of the Triune God. To worship the Father with the Son and in the Spirit is the true worship in the divine dispensing of the Divine Trinity.

III. THE WORSHIP IN THE DISPENSING OF GOD

When we speak of the worship in the dispensing of God, we are still speaking of our worship of the Father. The Jews, according to their view of the Old Testament, have their kind of worship of God. That is not the worship in God's dispensing. It is altogether not involved with the Triune God— the Father, the Son, and the Spirit. Basically speaking, the Jews know God only in His creation. They do not know God in His dispensing. They consider God as their Creator and they may even consider God as their Father in the sense of being their source but not in the sense of the Divine Trinity for the divine dispensing of Himself into our being.

In the Gospels there is only one chapter in which the Lord talked about the worship of God. When He talked about the worship of God in John 4, He was referring specifically to the worship of the Father. The Samaritan woman did not use the term *Father,* but she used the term *God.* Then the Lord Jesus told her, "But an hour is coming, and it is now, when the true worshippers will worship the Father in spirit and truthfulness, for the Father also seeks such to worship Him" (v. 23). This meant that the age had changed. Even when the Lord Jesus was talking to her, the age had changed, so the Lord used the term *Father,* saying that we need to worship the Father. When we use John 4:24, we usually neglect verse 23. The Lord did not say that we worship God but that we worship the Father. The Father seeks after this worship.

In verse 24 the Lord spoke of the nature of God. The nature of God is Spirit. The Lord did not say that we worship God but that we worship the Father, whose nature, as God, is Spirit. The worship here is absolutely different from the Jewish worship. The Jewish worship is altogether the worship of the Creator. But what the Lord spoke of is the worship of the Father in the Son and also in the Spirit. Thus, this is a worship in God's dispensing, the worship by the divine dispensing. When the Jews worship God as the Creator, they do not have the thought of God being dispensed into them. But if we would have the true worship, we need God to be dispensed into our being.

In John 4 the worship to the Father, the worship in the dispensing of God, is related to drinking the living water (vv. 10, 14). To contact God the Spirit with our spirit is to drink of the living water, and to drink of the living water is to render real worship to God. To expound John 4:24 we need John 4:14. We need to drink of the living water to worship the Father in spirit and in truthfulness. If we do not drink the living water, we do not drink of the Spirit (1 Cor. 12:13), we have no experience of God, and God is not dispensed into us.

Without drinking the living water, we cannot have a subjective worship in the divine dispensing. We can have only the Jewish kind of objective worship to an objective God as the Creator. Today our worship is subjective in the dispensing of God. Our worship is our experience of drinking the living water, the Spirit. In order to have the worship in the dispensing of God, we need to drink of the Spirit so that God may dispense Himself into our being. This is the new worship revealed in the New Testament.

Even today much of the worship in Christianity is actually

in the principle of the Jewish worship, the worship of the Creator who is far away from them. Our worship, however, is not merely to the Creator but to the Father, who has regenerated us and who has put Himself into our being. Now our worship is subjective with God—the Father, the Son, and the Spirit—dispensed into us.

This kind of worship can be practiced mostly in the Lord's table meeting, because in the Lord's table meeting, after we partake of the bread and the cup, the Lord takes the lead to bring us to the Father. The Lord leads us back to the Father in the Spirit. Here we must remember Ephesians 2:18, which reveals that our worship is through the Son, in the Spirit, and to the Father. This is fully portrayed in Luke 15 with the parables of the shepherd, the woman, and the father. It is through the Son's seeking as the shepherd and through the Spirit's enlightening as the woman that the prodigal son comes back to the Father. Therefore, this coming back to the Father is in the divine dispensing of the Divine Trinity. The Son and the Spirit are wrought into the returning son. This is the true worship in God's dispensing.

A. To Worship the Father

1. By Becoming the Father's Children

If we are to worship the Father, we first need to be reborn, becoming the Father's children (John 1:12; 1 John 3:1a).

2. By Knowing the Father's Name

In John 17:26a the Lord said that He would make the Father's name known to His disciples, and in Hebrews 2:12a we see that He declares the Father's name to His brothers. The name denotes the person. When you call on someone's name, the person comes, so the name of the Father denotes the Father's person. He is not only our God who created us but also the Father who begets us. He is not only the creating God but also the begetting Father. Now we are not only His creatures but also His children born of Him, begotten by Him. He is our Father, and we have to know His person. To know His person is to know His name.

All the disciples at that time had a Jewish background. They had the concept concerning God as their Creator, but they did not have any concept about God being their begetting Father. Before the Lord's resurrection, they did not have the concept that they were to be the children of God with God's life and nature. Before His resurrection, it was hard for the Lord to declare the Father's person to the disciples, because they did not have God as their Father. But in the resurrection He imparted the divine life into the disciples, so that made it easy for Him to make the Father's name, the Father's person, known to them.

On the day of His resurrection, He told Mary, "Go to My brothers and say to them, I ascend to My Father and your Father, and My God and your God" (John 20:17). The words *brothers* and *your Father* indicate an experience of life, a relationship in life. In His resurrection, the Lord imparted the Father's life and nature into the disciples. Now His Father is their Father and they are His brothers. This is all implied in knowing the Father's name, His person.

3. By Enjoying the Father's Presence

We worship the Father by enjoying the Father's presence. In John 14:23 the Lord said, "If anyone loves Me, he will keep My word, and My Father will love him, and We will come to him and make an abode with him." The Father and the Son will come to the one who loves the Son and will make Their abode with him. This is the constant presence of the Father. When we say, "Abba, Father" (Rom. 8:15; Gal. 4:6), we have a sweet inward sensation in an intimate enjoyment of the Father's presence.

By becoming the Father's children, by knowing the Father's name, and by enjoying the Father's presence, we worship the Father. If we are not born of the Father, do not know His person, and do not have His presence, we cannot worship Him subjectively. We can only worship an objective God.

B. In the Son as the Reality

We worship the Father in the Son as the reality (John 4:23-24). The Samaritan woman in John 4 tried to contend with the Lord Jesus by saying, "Our fathers worshipped in this mountain, yet you say that in Jerusalem is the place where men must worship" (v. 20). The Jews said this based upon Deuteronomy 12, which refers to Jerusalem as the unique place ordained by God for His people's worship. We have to refer the saints back to Deuteronomy 12 and tell them that the very worship ordained by God was with two regulations. First, it had to be in the unique, central place chosen by God, and second, it was with all the rich surplus of the produce of the good land. All the children of Israel in the ancient times had to worship God by keeping these two regulations.

The Lord pointed out to the Samaritan woman that the age had changed. Deuteronomy 12 was the typology, but in the New Testament we have the reality and the fulfillment. In typology the unique worship place was Jerusalem, and in the fulfillment this place is our spirit. Today our spirit is the actual Jerusalem where God's habitation is. Furthermore, the surplus of the produce of the good land was a type of the riches of Christ. Christ is the reality of all the offerings from the riches of the good land, including the burnt offering, the meal offering, the peace offering, the sin offering, the trespass offering, the wave offering, the heave offering, and the drink offering. All these offerings were the surplus of the produce of the good land as types of Christ who is the real surplus, the real offerings. Thus, in John 4:23-24 the human spirit replaces Jerusalem as the unique worship center and Christ replaces all the offerings, the surplus of the good land.

1. By Experiencing the Son as the Good Land

Our worship to the Father in the Son as the reality is by experiencing the Son as the good land (Deut. 8:7).

2. By Enjoying the Riches of the Son as the Rich Produce of the Good Land

We worship the Father in the Son as the reality by enjoying the riches of the Son as the rich produce of the good land (Deut. 8:8-10).

3. By Presenting the Son
to the Father as the Peace Offering

We worship the Father by presenting the Son to the Father as the peace offering (Lev. 3:1, 6, 12; 7:11-13).

C. In Our Spirit Mingled with the Spirit of God

We worship the Father in our spirit mingled with the Spirit of God (John 4:23-24).

1. By Being Born of the Spirit of God in Our Spirit

If we are going to worship God in our spirit, we must be born of the Spirit of God in our spirit (John 3:5, 6b). In John 3 there is the need to be born again, and in John 4 there is the worship in spirit. First, we need to be born of the Spirit, and then we can worship in spirit.

2. By Being Baptized into One Body
in the Spirit of God

By being baptized into one Body in the Spirit of God (1 Cor. 12:13a), we can worship the Father in our spirit. Actually, our worship in the dispensing of God is not an individual matter. According to the type in the Old Testament, all the children of Israel came to Jerusalem to worship, not in an individual way but in a corporate way. Their worship was corporate worship. At every feast, three times a year, they came together to worship God. Therefore, the worship in the dispensing of God according to the economy of God is a corporate worship in the Body.

3. By Drinking of the Spirit of God

We also worship in our spirit by drinking of the Spirit of God (1 Cor. 12:13b; John 4:14).

4. By Being in the Unique Place of Worship
Where God's Habitation Is

We must worship the Father by being in the unique place of worship where God's habitation is (Deut. 12:5; Eph. 2:22). After we are born of the Spirit of God in our spirit, baptized into one Body in the one Spirit, and drink of this one Spirit, our spirit becomes the unique place of worship because our spirit is the very place where God's habitation is. Christians are divided today because they will not come to their spirit to worship. If all the Christians would come to their spirit to worship, there would be no division. As long as all the children of Israel came to Jerusalem to worship, they were kept in oneness. The principle is the same today. Many Christians will not come to their regenerated spirit to worship God, so they are divided. Today we have to worship the Father in our spirit mingled with the Spirit of God.

D. In the Dispensing of the Triune God

Our worship to the Father in the Lord's table meeting is in the dispensing of the Triune God. We have been baptized into the Father, the Son, and the Holy Spirit (Matt. 28:19). We also enjoy the Father's love, the Son's grace, and the Spirit's fellowship (2 Cor. 13:14). We must be in the dispensing of the Triune God. Then we can have the proper and true worship in the divine dispensing of the Divine Trinity.

The focus of this message is as follows: the worship in the dispensing of the Triune God is the worship to the Father by His many sons with His firstborn Son as the offerings and in His Spirit who mingles Himself with our spirit as the unique place for our worship.

This fellowship should help us in the worship of the Father in the Lord's table meeting. This is the worship which the Lord revealed in John 4. John's Gospel tells us in chapter one that we have the right to be God's children. He gave as many as received Him the right, the authority, to be His children (v. 12). These children are born of God Himself. Then chapter three tells us how to be born of God. We must be born of water and the Spirit to be reborn of the Spirit (vv. 5-6). Chapter four goes on to reveal how to worship God as the Father in our spirit as the unique place of our worship and with the Son as the real offerings (vv. 23-24). We have to experience the dispensing of the Triune God—the Father, the Son, and the Spirit. Then we can have the kind of worship the Father seeks.

THE PRACTICE OF
THE LORD'S TABLE MEETING

(4)

Scripture Reading: Lev. 3:1-5, 6-7, 11, 12, 16; 7:11-13

OUTLINE

IV. Presenting Christ as the peace offering to the Father:
  A. The peace offering being the center of the basic offerings:
    1. From God's side based upon:
      a. The burnt offering—Lev. 1.
      b. The meal offering—Lev. 2.
    2. From our side based upon:
      a. The trespass offering—Lev. 5.
      b. The sin offering—Lev. 4.
  B. The required peace offering:
    1. An ox from the herd—Lev. 3:1.
    2. A sheep from the flock—Lev. 3:6.
    3. A lamb—Lev. 3:7.
    4. A goat—Lev. 3:12.
  C. The peace offering for thanksgiving—Lev. 7:12-13:
    1. With unleavened cakes mingled with oil.
    2. With unleavened wafers anointed with oil.
    3. With cakes of fine flour saturated and mingled with oil.
    4. In addition, with leavened bread.
Focus: When the problem of our trespass and sin is solved by Christ as the trespass offering and the sin offering, and when God and we are satisfied with Christ as the burnt offering and the meal offering, we can offer

Christ to God the Father as the peace offering for our mutual enjoyment in peace.

The presentation of Christ as the peace offering to God the Father as seen in Leviticus can be fulfilled in reality at the Lord's table meeting. In this presentation there are four main parties: God, the offerer, the serving priest, and the congregation of cleansed people. The peace offering is for the satisfaction of all four parties. The fat and the inward parts of the offering are God's portion (Lev. 3:3-5). The flesh, the meat, of the offering along with four kinds of cakes were the portion of the offerer (Lev. 7:12-13, 15-18). The four kinds of cakes and the right thigh as a heave offering were the portion of the serving priest (Lev. 7:14, 32-34), and the wave breast, typifying Christ as love in resurrection, were for all the priests (7:30-31, 34). Finally, the congregation's portion was the flesh of the cattle under the condition of cleanness (vv. 19-21).

This shows that as long as you come to the meeting, you still enjoy Christ as the portion common to all the saints. But if you offer Christ in the meeting and function as a serving priest, you enjoy a special portion. When we open up our mouth and function in the meeting, we are the serving priests presenting Christ to God the Father for His enjoyment and our enjoyment. Without this worship of the Father in the Lord's table meeting, the presentation of the peace offering to God cannot be fulfilled.

IV. PRESENTING CHRIST
AS THE PEACE OFFERING TO THE FATHER

We have to stress one point which all the saints at the Lord's table should know. This point is that there is no place other than the Lord's table meeting where the fulfillment of the peace offering can be accomplished. The fulfillment of the peace offering must be in the Lord's table meeting. After we eat the bread and drink the cup, the Lord takes the lead to come to the Father with all of us. He declares the Father's name to us and sings hymns of praise to the Father through us and with us (Heb. 2:12). At the same time, we offer Him as the peace offering to the Father. Then we and the Father, including all the serving ones, the offerers, and the congregation, enjoy Christ as the peace offering in a mutual way, not only in the presence of God the Father but also with God the Father.

A. The Peace Offering
Being the Center of the Basic Offerings

There are five basic offerings in the book of Leviticus: the burnt offering, the meal offering, the peace offering, the sin offering, and the trespass offering. The peace offering is in the middle, with two offerings before it and after it. Thus, it is the center of the basic offerings. It would be helpful to read the book entitled *Christ as the Reality* to see in more detail the significance of the five basic offerings in the book of Leviticus and the relation of the peace offering to the other four offerings.

1. From God's Side Based upon
the Burnt Offering and the Meal Offering

From God's side the peace offering is based upon the burnt offering (Lev. 1) and the meal offering (Lev. 2).

2. From Our Side Based upon
the Trespass Offering and the Sin Offering

From our side the peace offering is based upon the trespass offering (Lev. 5) and the sin offering (Lev. 4). The peace offering is the center of the basic offerings. From God's side, you have the burnt offering and the meal offering for the satisfaction both to God and to man. The experience of the peace offering is based mainly upon the burnt offering and the meal offering. Then from our side, the peace offering is based upon the trespass offering and the sin offering. On our side, there is the need of the trespass offering and the sin offering to take care of our trespasses and our sin. Then we can have peace with God.

B. The Required Peace Offering

The required peace offering was either an ox from the herd (Lev. 3:1), a sheep from the flock (v. 6), a lamb (v. 7, KJV), or a goat (v. 12). Here we have to tell the saints that Christ in Himself is the same, but Christ in our experience becomes different. Some experience Him in a rich way as a great ox; some experience Him as a sheep; some experience Him in a little way as a little lamb; and some even experience Him in a lesser way as a goat. The differences in the peace offering are not in Christ Himself but in our experience of Him. We offer Christ according to the measure and depth of our experience of Christ.

C. The Peace Offering for Thanksgiving

The peace offering is for our thanksgiving to the Father (Lev. 7:12-13). Because we are grateful to God the Father, we offer something of Christ as the peace offering to Him. We offer Christ as either an ox, a sheep, a lamb, or a goat with unleavened cakes mingled with oil. This is very meaningful. These unleavened cakes were thin cakes with holes. This means that they were easy to partake of and enjoy. The peace offering was also offered with unleavened, hollow wafers anointed with oil and with cakes of fine flour saturated and mingled with oil. The fine flour mingled with oil signifies Christ's humanity mingled with the Spirit. Christ's humanity mingled with divinity becomes a cake for our satisfaction.

When we offer the required peace offering for our thanksgiving, we need to add these cakes and wafers, which signify our experiences of Christ. This means we have to experience Christ in these three ways: Christ as the unleavened cakes mingled with oil, with the Spirit; Christ as the unleavened wafers anointed with oil, with the Spirit; and Christ as the cakes of fine flour saturated and mingled with oil, with the Spirit.

In addition to these cakes, the offerer also presented the peace offering to God with leavened bread. The leavened bread indicates that the presentation of Christ as the peace offering is initiated by us. Regardless of how spiritual we are, anything initiated by us has the element of sin, the element of leaven.

Leviticus 23 speaks of the Feast of Pentecost, in which two loaves of fine flour baked with leaven are offered to God (v. 17). These two loaves signify the two parts of the church as the Body of Christ, the Jewish part and the Gentile part, offered to God on the day of Pentecost. The two loaves are baked with leaven because both parts of the church are still sinful. In Christ Himself there is no leaven, but because we initiate this kind of thanksgiving offering, we bring in something unclean. This should help us to see that we should not have any trust in ourselves. Even in offering the peace offering for our thanksgiving toward God the Father, we are not clean because we are still in the flesh.

The focus of this lesson is as follows: when the problem of our trespass and sin is solved by Christ as the trespass offering and the sin offering, and when God and we are satisfied with Christ as the burnt offering and the meal offering, we can offer Christ to God the Father as the peace offering for our mutual enjoyment in peace.

The peace offering can be offered only after two things take place. First, on our side the problem of our trespass and sin should be solved by Christ as our trespass offering and as our sin offering. Second, God and we should be satisfied with Christ as the burnt offering and the meal offering. The burnt offering was fully for God, and the meal offering was for both God and man. When God and we are satisfied with Christ as the burnt offering and the meal offering, we can offer Christ as our peace offering for our mutual enjoyment in peace.

THE PRACTICE OF
THE LORD'S TABLE MEETING

(5)

Scripture Reading: Lev. 3:3-5, 9-11, 14-17; 7:11-21, 28-34

OUTLINE

IV. Presenting Christ as the peace offering to the Father:
  D. The portions of the peace offering:
    1. To God:
      a. From the ox—3:3-5:
        1) The fat upon the inwards.
        2) The two kidneys and the fat on them.
        3) The caul (net) above the liver.
      b. From the sheep or lamb—3:9-11:
        1) The same as from the ox.
        2) Plus the whole fat tail.
      c. From the goat—the same as from the ox—3:14-16.
    2. To the offering priest:
      a. One cake as a heave offering unto the Lord—7:14.
      b. The right thigh as a heave offering unto the Lord—7:32-34.
    3. To all the priests—the breast as a wave offering—7:30-31, 34.
    4. To the offerer:
      a. The flesh (meat) of the cattle—7:15-18:
        1) Of the peace offering for thanksgiving good for eating on the offering day—v. 15.

        2) Of the peace offering for a vow or a voluntary offering good for eating for two days—vv. 16-18.

    b. Cakes—7:12-13:

        1) Unleavened cakes—thin cakes with holes—mingled with oil.

        2) Unleavened, hollow wafers anointed with oil.

        3) Cakes of fine flour saturated and mingled with oil.

        4) Leavened bread.

  5. To others—7:19-21:

    a. The flesh of the cattle.

    b. Cleanness being required.

Focus: Christ as the peace offering offered by us to the Father is for the enjoyment of God and all the parties participating in the worship in the dispensing of God.

In this lesson we want to continue our fellowship concerning presenting Christ as the peace offering to the Father in the Lord's table meeting. In particular we want to see the significance of the portions of the peace offering as seen in Leviticus.

D. The Portions
of the Peace Offering

1. To God

a. From the Ox

A portion of the peace offering is presented to God from the ox (Lev. 3:3-5). This portion is the fat upon the inwards, the inner parts, of the cattle. All the fat upon all the inwards must be for God. The two kidneys and the fat on them is for God, as well as the caul (net) above the liver. All this fat and these tender parts within the cattle must be burned to God as His food to satisfy Him and to please Him.

These items refer to the sweetness and the tenderness of the inward being of Christ. The inward being of Christ can be appreciated only by God. We do not have that much ability in our apprehension. In our apprehension we cannot perceive that deeply. Only God has such an appreciating ability. In Matthew 11:27 the Lord Jesus said that "no one fully knows the Son except the Father." When He said this, a number of people, including the disciples, were around Him. They saw Him, but they could not perceive what was within His inward being. No human being can fully perceive what is in the Lord's inward being. Only God can fully evaluate it, appreciate it, enjoy it, and apprehend it.

Leviticus does not say that the heart is offered to God for His portion. Instead, it emphatically mentions the kidneys and the liver when speaking of the portions of the peace offering which are God's portion. There is no fat around the heart. If there were, that would be terrible. Of course, the heart is a vitally crucial organ, but the liver and kidneys are very tender and very sensitive. This is a picture of what is within Christ which is invisible, or unseen, to human eyes. Only God can perceive what is there.

The fat always indicates sweetness and tenderness. The softest, sweetest, and most tender part in the cattle is the fat, which becomes food to God through burning. The best part of the cattle for burning is the fat. It would be against the "medical law" for the priests to eat the fat. It is altogether unhealthy for us humans to eat fat, but it is altogether healthy to God. We cannot digest the fat, but God can. Fat gives us trouble, but fat does not give any trouble to God. The divine digestion is different from our human digestion.

This shows us how marvelous the Bible is. They did not have the benefit of modern science in the days of the Old Testament, but God established a dietary ordinance for the priests according to His medical law. Modern science, of course, has discovered that fat is not good for the human body. But in the Bible, this principle was there already. God kept all the fat away from the priests.

Many of the Chinese eat all the fat. They treasure the fat and give it to the people whom they respect. But the Jews in the Old Testament offered all the fat to God, and God could digest it. This is very meaningful. Because many of the Chinese do not know God, they give the wrong thing to the wrong persons. But the Jews in the Old Testament knew God according to the Scriptures, so they offered the right thing to the right person, that is, God. The fat of the cattle must go to God.

b. From the Sheep or Lamb

The portions of the peace offering which are offered to God are also from the sheep or lamb (Lev. 3:9-11). These portions are the same as from the ox plus the whole fat tail. The King James Version uses the word *rump*, but the Hebrew word means *fat tail*. The American Standard Version says that the entire "fat tail" of the peace offering is offered to God. The fat tail and the fat upon the inwards again refer to the sweet and tender parts of Christ's being. No human can apprehend this portion. It can be realized and enjoyed only by the Father.

c. From the Goat

The portions of the peace offering offered to God from the goat are the same as from the ox (3:14-16). All these portions, signifying the tender, sweet, and delicious parts of Christ, are for God. They are God's portion.

2. To the Offering Priest

This is the second category of the portions of the peace offering. The first is the portion to God, and the second is the portion to the offering priest.

a. One Cake as a Heave Offering unto the Lord

When the children of Israel offered a peace offering according to God's requirements, they did not need to offer any cakes. God required only the cattle for the peace offering. But if the offerer was thankful to God and offered it for a thanksgiving, he had to add something to the required peace offering. This portion is composed not of the cattle but of the cakes. According to Leviticus 7:14, out of the many cakes offered, one had to be set apart and heaved unto God as a heave offering. This became the portion of the offering priest, the conducting and serving priest, the priest who offered the blood and the fat.

Leviticus 7:13 and 14 say, "With the thanksgiving sacrifice of his peace offering, he shall offer his offering with cakes of leavened bread; and from it he shall offer one from each offering as a heave offering to Jehovah; it shall be for the priest who dashes the blood of the peace offering." Every time the serving priest offered a peace offering for thanksgiving, he had to take out one cake for a heave offering. If he offered an offering, he had to take out one piece from all the cakes and heave it unto the Lord. Then this piece would become his portion.

b. The Right Thigh as a Heave Offering unto the Lord

The right thigh of the peace offering was also given to the priest for a heave offering out of the sacrifices of the peace offerings (Lev. 7:32-34). The one cake and the right thigh were for nourishing and strengthening the serving priest. The cake was for nourishing, the thigh was for strengthening, and both were heave offerings. This refers to the enjoyment of the ascension of Christ, to enjoying Christ as the ascended One, the heaved One. This shows that the offering priests, the conducting priests, get the highest enjoyment. The more we serve, the higher the portion of Christ we enjoy.

3. To All the Priests—
the Breast as a Wave Offering

The breast as a wave offering was a portion of the peace offering to all the priests, including Aaron and all his sons (Lev. 7:30-31, 34). The wave offering is not as high as the heave offering, and the breast is not as strong as the thigh. Thus, all the priests share a portion which is not as high or as strong as that which the serving priests share. The highest and strongest portion is for the serving priests, not for the general priests. The general priests share only a kind of general portion. They share the wave breast, not the heave thigh. The wave offering signifies the resurrected Christ. The heave offering signifies the exalted Christ. The exalted Christ, of course, is higher than the resurrected Christ. Until we experience Christ in ascension, we have not reached the goal. We are still on the way.

The breast does not signify strength; it signifies love. This indicates that as long as the church is still in the stage of love it is not so strong and somewhat low. The church must go on from the stage of love to the stage of strength, that is, from the breast stage to the thigh stage. If there are many general priests among us and few serving priests, our church life will be weak. We need some particular serving ones to enjoy the right thigh as a heave offering.

4. To the Offerer

A portion of the peace offering also goes to the offerer.

a. The Flesh (Meat) of the Cattle

The flesh (meat) of the cattle is the portion to the offerer

(7:15-18). The flesh of the peace offering for thanksgiving is good for eating on the offering day (v. 15), whereas the flesh of the peace offering for a vow or a voluntary offering is good for eating for two days (vv. 16-18). This shows that the offering for a vow is stronger than the offering for thanksgiving. Thus, the offering for thanksgiving is good to eat for only one day. But the offering for a vow or a voluntary offering is stronger, so it can last for two days.

We need to see the difference between the peace offering for thanksgiving and the peace offering for a vow. The offering for a vow is stronger. Today we may consecrate ourselves to God with thanksgiving. We may pray, "Lord, I love You, so I consecrate myself to You." This is for thanksgiving, but this is too general. On the other hand, we may offer ourselves to God with a vow. We may pray, "Lord, I come here to make a vow to You. I give myself to You and marry myself to You. I want to be solely for You always, regardless of what happens or of how I feel." A vow is something voluntary.

A number of saints may consecrate themselves to Christ and the church, but five years later they may leave the church. This means that they did not have a vow. A vow is like a marriage tie. The offering for thanksgiving, though, is based upon our feeling. We may stay with someone because of our feeling of love for them, but a vow goes beyond our feeling. It is a tie that binds us regardless of feeling or circumstance. All of us need to be ones who are married to Christ for His recovery. Then regardless of what happens or of how we feel, we will always remain with the Lord for His recovery. I am grateful to the Lord that many saints are really bound to Christ by a marriage vow. To make such a vow is to be a real Nazarite according to what is revealed in Numbers 6.

The offering for thanksgiving is emotional and superficial, but the offering for a vow is determined and deeper. Thanksgiving is mostly related to the emotion, but a vow is related to the will. Some saints' consecrations are out of thanksgiving, whereas others' consecrations are out of a vow. In order to follow the Lord, we need a vow. Marriage involves a vow with no change, no variation, no alteration. The Lord treasures our vow to Him.

b. Cakes

Besides the meat of the cattle, the offerer also enjoys three kinds of cakes as his portion (7:12-13).

1) Unleavened Cakes—Thin Cakes with Holes— Mingled with Oil

First, there are unleavened cakes mingled with oil. Darby points out in a note on Leviticus 2:4 that these cakes are very thin with holes. Their being thin and perforated makes them easier to eat and digest. This is a type of Christ as the One who is easy to eat and digest. He is mingled with the Spirit, and He is unleavened, without any sin.

2) Unleavened, Hollow Wafers Anointed with Oil

The second kind of cake is the unleavened, hollow wafers anointed with oil. These wafers are also easy to eat, digest, and enjoy because they are empty, hollow, within. The unleavened cakes are mingled with oil, whereas the unleavened, hollow wafers are anointed with oil.

Christ was always hollow within; to be hollow means to be poor in spirit. Furthermore, He was pierced on the cross, that is, He was perforated. Many Christians today are like a cake twelve inches thick, without one hole. No one can eat of them. But Christ was not that thick. Christ made Himself so humble. He was hollow, poor in spirit, and perforated, pierced, for our enjoyment.

3) Cakes of Fine Flour Saturated and Mingled with Oil

The third kind of cake is of fine flour saturated and mingled with oil. To be mingled is one thing, to be saturated is another thing, and to be anointed is still another thing. For the cake to be mingled with oil is something within. For the cake to be saturated with oil is for it to be soaked with oil. For the cake to be anointed with oil is for the oil to be poured upon it.

These cakes were to be offered with the sacrifice of

thanksgiving, which is something we add to what God requires. God is satisfied with the required ox, the required sheep, the required lamb, or the required goat. But when we are so grateful for what we have enjoyed of Christ, we have something to give to God for our thanksgiving. This is an experience of Christ in addition to what God requires and is initiated by us. Because we are so grateful to God for Christ, we bring something additional of Christ to God.

Of course, what Christ has done for us in His redemption is altogether included in the cattle. We cannot add anything to this. But still the cattle does not include Christ's behavior, Christ's human life. We need to read the four Gospels to realize Christ's human living on this earth. He is typified by the cakes of the peace offering, which were thin and hollow. When we are grateful to God, we bring something of Christ in the aspect of His human living as our gratitude to God.

4) Leavened Bread

Leviticus 7:13 says, "With the thanksgiving sacrifice of his peace offering, he shall offer his offering with cakes of leavened bread." The other items are for appreciation and enjoyment, whereas the leaven reminds us that we, the offerers and enjoyers of such a holy Christ, are still unholy; we are still leavened. Whatever God does is absolutely pure and holy. But whatever we initiate still has some leaven in it. The leavened bread reminds the offerer that he is still sinful. Whenever we offer Christ at the Lord's table, we need to be reminded that we are still unclean, still leavened.

5. To Others

a. The Flesh of the Cattle

There are five parties participating in the five portions of the peace offering. One portion is to God, one portion is to the conducting priest, one portion is to all the priests, one portion is to the offerer, and the last portion is to others, that is, to the rest of the congregation who are worshipping God (7:19-21). The last portion to others is the flesh of the cattle. Of course, no offerer by himself can eat all the offerings, so some "eating helpers" are needed. This is why we all come together at the Lord's table to enjoy the unsearchably rich Christ.

Today we ourselves must be the conducting priests, the serving priests. In the Old Testament worship, there were the serving priests and the ones who came to them to offer something. But in the New Testament there are no clergy and laity. Today we must be all four parties: the offerers, the conducting priests, the general priests, and the congregation. Only certain portions of the peace offering, mostly the inward parts, are for God, but the rest are for us.

Some among us, however, may come to the meeting merely as a part of the congregation and not as offerers. Others may be offerers, but they are not that strong and there is not the real serving priesthood with them. Doctrinally speaking, there are no clergy and laity among us. But actually some may offer a "layman's" prayer, whereas others may offer a serving one's prayer. We can discern the difference. We are all priests, but some may be lazy and will not serve. These ones can enjoy only the wave breast, not the heave thigh. This typology in Leviticus presents a full picture of today's situation.

b. Cleanness Being Required

Anyone who wants to eat the peace offering must be clean, without sin. This is fully dealt with in 1 Corinthians 11, which points out that it is possible for us to partake of the Lord's table in an unworthy manner (v. 27). First Corinthians 5 tells us what kinds of persons are unclean and should be excluded from the fellowship of the Lord's Body.

The focus of this lesson is as follows: Christ as the peace offering offered by us to the Father is for the enjoyment of God and all the parties participating in the worship in the dispensing of God.

THE PRACTICE OF
THE LORD'S TABLE MEETING

(6)

Scripture Reading: Lev. 3:1-17; 7:23, 25-27, 33

OUTLINE

IV. Presenting Christ as the peace offering to the Father:
   E. The enjoyment of the peace offering:
      1. God's portion:
         a. The blood—3:2, 8, 13, 17; 7:26-27, 33:
            1) To satisfy His righteous requirements.
            2) To maintain His holy position.
            3) To keep His glory—cf. Rom. 3:23.
         b. The fat—3:3-4, 9-10, 14-17; 7:23, 25, 33:
            1) The inward riches for His satisfaction according to His glory.
            2) The protection of the inwards.
         c. The two kidneys—the most tender part of the inwards—3:4, 10, 15.
         d. The net above the liver—3:4, 10, 15:
            1) The additional inward riches.
            2) The covering of the inward part.
         e. The fat tail of the sheep or the lamb—the additional riches—3:9.
         f. A sweet savor made by fire of items b through e as food to God—3:5, 11, 16.

In the previous lesson we saw the portions of the peace offering. In this lesson we want to begin to fellowship about the enjoyment of the peace offering. For this lesson we need to read all of Leviticus 3. I feel that we need to help the saints to read this chapter very carefully, and we need to ask them to pay their full attention to two things: the blood and the fat. We have seen that the net above the liver is also God's portion from the peace offering. The net is a part of the fat. In addition to this, there are the two kidneys and the fat tail. Actually, the fat tail is additional fat (Lev. 3:9).

E. The Enjoyment of the Peace Offering

1. God's Portion

a. The Blood

In this lesson we want to cover God's portion of the enjoyment of the peace offering. God's portion firstly is the blood (Lev. 3:2, 8, 13, 17; 7:26-27, 33). The fat is for God, and the blood is also for God. Men were not allowed to eat the fat or to drink the blood. Leviticus 3:17 says, "It shall be a perpetual statute throughout your generations wherever you dwell, that you shall not eat any fat or any blood." This verse strongly charges that no fat or blood should be taken by anyone.

1) To Satisfy His Righteous Requirements

The blood satisfies God's righteous requirements. God needs the blood. God desires to have fellowship with His chosen people, but He is righteous. His righteous requirements will not allow Him to have fellowship with His chosen people as long as they have sins. Therefore, the blood is required. We may say that our sin or our sins require the blood, but actually, it is not so accurate to say this. The most we can say is that our sin or our sins need the blood to solve their problem. But the requirements are not on our side; the requirements are on God's side. God's righteous requirements need the blood. So the blood firstly satisfies God's righteous requirements.

2) To Maintain His Holy Position

Righteousness is a condition, whereas holiness is a position. The blood is needed to satisfy God's righteousness, and it is also needed to maintain God's holiness, God's holy position. If God came to fellowship with us sinners without the blood, this would overthrow His position. He is the holy God, and His position is altogether holy, separated from anything common.

3) To Keep His Glory

The requirements of God's righteousness, God's holiness, and God's glory all need to be met. Glory is the expression of God in His dignity. God's righteous condition should be satisfied, God's holy position should be maintained, and God's glory, that is, His expressed dignity, should be kept. The blood of Christ satisfies God's righteous requirements, maintains God's holy position, and keeps God's glorious dignity, so the blood is God's portion.

b. The Fat

1) The Inward Riches for His Satisfaction according to His Glory

The fat is also God's portion (Lev. 3:3-4, 9-10, 14-17; 7:23, 25, 33). The fat signifies the inward riches for God's satisfaction according to His glory. This corresponds with the revelation in the New Testament of the unsearchable riches of Christ (Eph. 3:8). Also, in John 10:10 the Lord said that He came that we might have life abundantly. The fat signifies the abundance of life.

2) The Protection of the Inwards

According to the record of Leviticus 3, the fat is upon the inward parts. Thus, we may say that the inward riches are the covering for and the protection of the inward parts. The inward parts of the peace offering signify the inward parts, the inward being, of Christ (Phil. 1:8). The four Gospels show us what was within the Lord Jesus while He was living, walking, and working on this earth. By reading the four

Gospels, we can realize that the Lord's thought, His desire, His intention, His love, His likes and dislikes, His emotions, and all the things within Him were very tender and very rich toward God and in the presence of God. By reading the biography of the Lord Jesus in the four Gospels, we can realize that within Him were the rich and tender inward parts. All His inward parts are very tender, very rich, and very precious.

In the Lord's table meeting, after the remembrance of the Lord, we should offer the Lord as the peace offering to the Father. What we offer should include, or comprise, the inward parts of Christ. Now we need to consider whether we offer an objective peace offering or a subjective peace offering. In other words, do we offer something produced merely by God or produced by ourselves. According to the typology, the peace offerings were offered by the producers. They produced the cattle and the other items of their offerings. This shows that we have to labor on Christ as the good land.

Of course, according to the Old Testament, some people did not labor but bought something to offer. They took advantage of others' labor. But these offerings which were bought were not as sweet as those produced by the people's labor. The best and sweetest offerings are those produced by ourselves. If I do not labor on Christ, yet I offer the Christ you labor on, this is not so good. I must offer what I have labored on. I must offer what is produced by my labor, and you must offer what is produced by your labor.

The fat on the inwards offered to God should be something produced by us. In other words, if we do not have the kind of tender, rich, and precious intention, will, desire, and purpose in our daily life that Christ had, it will be hard for us to present Christ to the Father in this way at the Lord's table meeting. If in our daily walk we are really one with the Lord in our intention toward the Father, in our concept, in our thoughts, in our likes and dislikes, in our desire, in our intent, and in our purpose, then these things become our experience. Then we are really one with the Lord in His inward parts toward the Father. If this is the case, we have the reality of the inwards and the fat upon the inwards of the peace offering when we come to the Lord's table meeting.

Those in the Pentecostal movement care only for their power, their revivals, and for something great. Nearly everything with them is rough and outward. For the most part, they do not care for the inward parts of Christ, the inward being of Christ, as typified by the kidneys and the fat upon the inwards. In the Pentecostal movement, there is nothing hidden, nothing covered. But when we read the four Gospels, we can see that the life of Jesus was very much an inward matter. Within Him the divine riches were concealed, hidden. If we are outward like those in Pentecostalism, we will not have the inwards when we come to offer the peace offering.

c. The Two Kidneys— the Most Tender Part of the Inwards

Now we need to consider what the two kidneys signify (Lev. 3:4, 10, 15). Of all the inward parts, the kidneys are among the smallest. Furthermore, the kidneys are the most tender of the inward parts. This indicates that we need some small yet most tender things within us toward God the Father. Within us God does not want big things. Within us the Father wants small things which are very tender and precious. The kidneys are protected by the fat, which means that the small yet tender and precious things within us toward the Father are protected by the inward riches.

What we are speaking of here is altogether based upon our experiences. If we do not have the rich experiences of life, we cannot have the small, tender, and precious things within us toward God the Father. With the inwards, which are so sweet to the Father, the size means nothing, but the quantity does. The more fat there is, the better. With the life of the Lord Jesus in the four Gospels, there were the riches, the abundance in quantity, but there was no greatness in size.

An illustration of this can be seen in John 7. In this chapter the Lord's brothers in the flesh told Him to go to Judea and manifest Himself to the world (vv. 3-4), but the Lord responded by saying, "My time has not yet come, but your time is always ready" (v. 6). Such an instance shows us the tenderness, the preciousness, and the riches of life within the Lord. His life was not one of a great work, a great career, or a great activity. Although He was the Son of the Almighty God, He was willing to be limited in not doing anything. His brothers in the flesh challenged Him to manifest Himself publicly, to do something great to make a name, but He said His time had not yet come. He liked to be small. In His life with the Father, there was an inward restriction. This shows us the kidneys of the peace offering offered to the Father with the smallness, the tenderness, and the preciousness.

No human word can adequately express this revelation, but this instance in John 7 shows us the Lord's inward being as typified by the kidneys of the peace offering with the fat around them. If we are great, spiritual giants according to the way of today's Christianity, we will not be able to offer the fat with the two kidneys. If we read the four Gospels to see the life of Jesus, we can see His inward being as typified by the inward parts of the peace offering. We can see that His inward being was rich in life with something tender and small, yet so precious to God the Father. This fully corresponds with our experiences. This indicates that strength and power signified by the thigh do not satisfy the Father. The Father desires the inward parts of Christ signified by the fat and the kidneys.

d. The Net above the Liver

The net above the liver (Lev. 3:4, 10, 15), not the liver itself, was offered to God as the additional inward riches and the covering of this inward part. I believe that the liver was not required because it was not as small as the kidneys. The net above the liver is thinner than the fat surrounding the other parts. Of course, a net cannot be that thick. This means that the liver is not only bigger than the kidneys but also not as greatly protected by the fat. But regardless of how thin the net is, it is still the fat, and the fat is required as God's portion. This shows that we must have the riches of life to protect and to keep our experiences of the inward parts of Christ, which are so precious to God the Father. Within us we may have some experiences of the inward being of Christ, but we may not have that much of the riches of life. The net of the liver is thin, but it still functions as the additional inward riches to cover the liver.

e. The Fat Tail of the Sheep or the Lamb—
the Additional Riches

The fat tail of the sheep or the lamb was also God's portion of the peace offering as additional riches (Lev. 3:9). With the sheep or the lamb, the riches of life as the fat tail are outside of the inwards. This indicates that the sheep or the lamb, according to the fat, is better than the ox because the ox's fat tail is not accepted. It is not tender enough.

The fat, the kidneys, the net above the liver, and the fat tail all indicate the riches of life inwardly with the tenderness, the smallness, and the preciousness. If we want to do a great work, make a great name, or have a great success right away, there can be no inwards in our offering to God. In other words, there can be no riches stored, concealed, or hidden inwardly. There can be nothing small, tender, and precious for God the Father.

I do not have the human language to adequately express this, but I would repeatedly refer you to the life of the Lord Jesus in the four Gospels. The life in the Gospels is sweeter and more tender than the life revealed in Acts. The life in the Gospels has more fat and inwards. I am not depreciating the life in Acts, but nothing can compare with the life of the Lord Jesus Himself revealed in the Gospels. The life in the Gospels is richer, more tender, more precious, and yet smaller. Which do you appreciate more—the three thousand saved on the day of Pentecost in Acts 2 or the three disciples on the high mountain with the Lord Jesus in Matthew 17? Do you want to be among the three or merely among the three thousand? Pentecostal preachers would prefer the three thousand. But what happened with the three thousand was not even as high in a certain sense as what took place with the five thousand who were fed by the Lord in the Gospels (Matt. 14:14-21). This shows that in the Gospels there are more inwards with more fat.

f. A Sweet Savor Made by Fire
of Items b through e as Food to God

The portions of the peace offering which are God's portion become a sweet savor made by fire as food to God (Lev. 3:5, 11, 16). It is a sweet savor made by fire of the fat, the kidneys, the net above the liver, and the fat tail. These four items burned by fire produce the savor, and this savor is food to God (3:5, 11, 16). This is God's enjoyment of the peace offering. Whether or not we can offer such a peace offering depends upon our daily walk.

THE PRACTICE OF
THE LORD'S TABLE MEETING

(7)

Scripture Reading: Lev. 7:11-21, 28-34

OUTLINE

IV. Presenting Christ as the peace offering to the Father:
  E. The enjoyment of the peace offering:
    2. The offering priest's portion:
      a. One cake out of each of the following as a heave offering unto Jehovah—Christ in His humanity as nourishment in ascension to the serving one—7:14:
        1) Unleavened, perforated, thin cakes mingled with oil—Christ living a crucified life mingled with the Spirit and easy to be contacted and received—7:12a.
        2) Unleavened, hollow wafers anointed with oil—Christ living a humble life under the anointing of the Spirit—7:12b; Phil. 2:7-8.
        3) Cakes of fine flour saturated and mingled with oil—Christ living a fine human life saturated and mingled with the Spirit—7:12c.
        4) Leavened bread, signifying the sinfulness of the offerer and the offering priest as a reminder to them—7:13.
      b. The right thigh as a heave offering unto Jehovah—the power of Christ in ascension

for the strengthening of the serving one—
7:32-34.

3. The priesthood's portion—the breast as a wave
offering before Jehovah—the love of Christ
in resurrection for nourishment to all the
priests—7:30-31, 34.

4. The offerer's portion:

   a. The flesh of the cattle—the supply of
Christ—7:15-18:

      1) Of the peace offering for thanksgiving
(of emotion) good for eating for one
day—v. 15.

      2) Of the peace offering for a vow or a
voluntary offering (of the will) good for
eating for two days—vv. 16-18.

   b. Cakes of all four kinds as described in 1),
2), 3), and 4), under 2a—Christ in His
humanity as food to His offerer—7:12-13.

5. The congregation's portion—7:19-21:

   a. The flesh of the cattle—the supply of Christ
for nourishment.

   b. Under the condition of cleanness—1 Cor.
5:8-11, 13b.

In this lesson we want to continue our fellowship concerning the enjoyment of the peace offering. We have seen that God's portion of the peace offering is mainly of two things: the blood and the fat. We have to realize that these two things are of great significance. This is because the Bible reveals that our relationship with God is always based upon three of His attributes: the righteousness of God, the holiness of God, and the glory of God. According to the whole Bible, the relationship we have with God must be based upon or built on these three divine attributes.

The whole book of Romans was constructed with these three elements or attributes. The first section of Romans is concerning justification, and justification is according to God's righteousness. Then the second section of Romans covers the matter of sanctification, and sanctification is by the holiness of God. Then Romans has another section concerning glorification. We have been justified; we are now being sanctified; and some day we will be glorified with God's glory. Romans is constructed with God's righteousness, holiness, and glory because it is a book that shows us the real relationship between God and us. This relationship is based upon and built on God's righteousness for justification, God's holiness for sanctification, and God's glory for glorification. When these three things of God are taken care of in a good way, then there is no problem in our relationship with God.

All the offerings in their reality are for our relationship with God, so in these offerings, the crucial items to God are the blood and the fat. The blood meets the requirements of God's righteousness and holiness, and it also maintains God's glory. Romans 3:23 says that all have sinned and fall short of the glory of God. The cleansing power of the blood keeps God's glory from being insulted by sin. Instead of expressing God in His glory, man expresses sin and his sinful self. Hence, man falls short of God's glory. This falling short of God's glory and expression is sin. The blood cleanses us from every sin (1 John 1:7) and thus maintains the glory of God.

Then there is the need of the fat on the positive side to

satisfy God's desire unto God's glory. The fat is to satisfy God's desire, whereas the blood is to meet His requirements. The fat signifies Christ's inward riches for God's satisfaction according to His glory and up to the standard of His glory. God's satisfaction issues in God's glory. This implies that the fat fulfills God's purpose. The fat is the inward riches of the cattle offered as a sacrifice, and this signifies the riches of the inward life of Christ. This life satisfies God the Father and fulfills God's eternal purpose.

Also, this life has the abundance of riches which preserves the inward functions, typified by the liver and the kidneys. The inward functions are all preserved, protected, and covered by the riches of life. According to our own experiences, we can realize this and testify to this. If we are short of the riches of life, our inward functions become rough, numb, and dull. The more riches of life we have, the more our inward functions become so tender, fresh, new, and living. This shows us that the riches of the inward life of the Lord Jesus preserved His inward functions for them to be so tender and fresh to the Father. This all satisfies the Father's desire unto His glory.

Thus, we can see that by the blood and the fat of the peace offering, God's requirements are taken care of and God's desire is satisfied. Then nothing insults God's glory, but instead God is expressed in His glory. Actually, the blood and the fat should be the essential elements of our service today, with the blood taking care of all God's requirements and the fat taking care of God's desire unto His glory.

2. The Offering Priest's Portion

Leviticus 7:12 through 14 says, "If he offers it for thanksgiving, then with the thanksgiving sacrifice he shall offer unleavened cakes mingled with oil, and unleavened wafers anointed with oil, and cakes of fine flour saturated, mingled with oil. With the thanksgiving sacrifice of his peace offering, he shall offer his offering with cakes of leavened bread; and from it he shall offer one from each offering as a heave offering to Jehovah; it shall be for the priest who dashes the blood of the peace offering." Out of the many cakes offered, one of each kind had to be set apart and heaved unto God as a heave offering. This became the portion of the serving priest.

a. One Cake out of Each of the Following as a Heave Offering unto Jehovah— Christ in His Humanity as Nourishment in Ascension to the Serving One

All the cakes are types of Christ in His humanity, and these become a heave offering to Jehovah. This shows that Christ in His humanity becomes nourishment in ascension to us, the serving ones.

1) Unleavened, Perforated, Thin Cakes Mingled with Oil—Christ Living a Crucified Life Mingled with the Spirit and Easy to Be Contacted and Received

The unleavened, perforated, thin cakes mingled with oil signify Christ living a crucified life mingled with the Spirit and easy to be contacted and received (Lev. 7:12a). The thin cakes are easy to eat, meaning that Christ is easy to be contacted and received. If a cake is too thick, it is hard to eat. These cakes are also perforated, pierced through. This indicates the dealing of the cross and signifies the crucified life.

The four Gospels show us that the Lord's life on this earth was "full of holes." His life was a perforated life, a crucified life. He was living a life which was always pierced through by some sufferings. Furthermore, the four Gospels show us that Christ was easy to be contacted and received, as typified by the thinness of the unleavened cakes. These cakes were mingled with oil, signifying that Christ was mingled with the Spirit.

2) Unleavened, Hollow Wafers Anointed with Oil— Christ Living a Humble Life under the Anointing of the Spirit

The second kind of cake is the unleavened, hollow wafers anointed with oil (Lev. 7:12b). The Lord in His human life on this earth was very hollow, which means that He was poor in spirit; He was humble (Phil. 2:7-8). He lived such a humble life under the anointing of the Spirit. The mingling of the

Spirit was within Him, and the anointing of the Spirit was upon Him.

In the four Gospels, we can see these two aspects of the Lord Jesus' life. His life was on the one hand mingled with the Spirit. When He was twelve years old in the temple, we can see the mingling within Him but not the anointing upon Him (Luke 2:40-52). But in Luke 4 we can see the anointing. In verse 18 the Lord quoted from the book of Isaiah: "The Spirit of the Lord is upon Me, because He has anointed Me..." (Isa. 61:1-2). By reading the four Gospels, we can see that some instances of the Lord's life show a life mingled with the Spirit and others show a life under the anointing of the Spirit.

3) Cakes of Fine Flour Saturated and Mingled with Oil— Christ Living a Fine Human Life Saturated and Mingled with the Spirit

The fine flour always signifies the Lord's fine and balanced human life. It was so even; it was not coarse or unbalanced. His human life is composed of and is constituted with the element of fine flour. These cakes of fine flour were saturated and mingled with oil (Lev. 7:12c). Being saturated is deeper than being mingled. You may have something mingled and yet it may not be saturated. The anointing is without, the mingling is within, and the saturating is the soaking and penetrating of the oil into the fine flour. This shows us how detailed the Bible is. The anointing, mingling, and saturating tell us that the Lord's human living on this earth was not only outwardly under the Spirit but also mingled with the Spirit to the extent that His whole human element was saturated and soaked with the Spirit.

4) Leavened Bread, Signifying the Sinfulness of the Offerer and the Offering Priest as a Reminder to Them

Leviticus 7:13 says, "With the thanksgiving sacrifice of his peace offering, he shall offer his offering with cakes of leavened bread." The leavened bread here according to typology is a reminder that both the offerer and the conducting priest are still sinful.

b. The Right Thigh as a Heave Offering
unto Jehovah—the Power of Christ in Ascension
for the Strengthening of the Serving One

The portion of the offering priest is also the right thigh as a heave offering to Jehovah (Lev. 7:32-34). The right side in the Bible always indicates the highest position. The right thigh as a heave offering signifies the power of Christ in ascension, the power of the One who is in the highest position, seated at the right hand of God.

Resurrection mainly refers to life. Ascension refers to power. On the day of resurrection, the Lord breathed the Spirit into the disciples; that was the Spirit of life (John 20:22). Then on the day of Pentecost in His ascension, He poured out the Spirit of power, which was symbolized by the mighty wind (Acts 2:2). The Spirit of life is breath, and the Spirit of power is the mighty wind. The breath gives life and the wind is powerful. The day of resurrection was a day of breath, a day of life, but the day of Pentecost was a day of wind, a day of power.

The right thigh is offered as a heave offering. This indicates the power of Christ in His ascension for the strengthening of the serving one. Therefore, the two main portions for the enjoyment of the priests who conduct the offering are the cakes for their nourishment and the right thigh for their strengthening. This means that in our service we need the nourishment and the power. We need the cakes and the right thigh. We need the cakes typifying the crucified human life of Jesus, the humble human life of Jesus, and the saturated human life of Jesus as our nourishment for our service, and we also need the right thigh to empower us for our service.

3. The Priesthood's Portion—the Breast
as a Wave Offering before Jehovah—
the Love of Christ in Resurrection
for Nourishment to All the Priests

The priesthood's portion refers to the portion for the body of the priests. The word *priesthood* has two meanings. It means the priestly service, the priestly ministry, and also the priestly body, the corporate body of priests. Here the priesthood refers to the priestly body.

The priesthood's portion, the portion for the whole body of priests, was the breast as a wave offering before Jehovah (Lev. 7:30-31, 34). For the heave offering, the preposition is *unto,* that is, it is heaved *unto* Jehovah. For the wave offering, the preposition is *before,* that is, it is waved *before* Jehovah. The Lord Jesus was *before* the Father in His resurrection and *unto* the Father in His ascension. The breast as a wave offering before Jehovah signifies the love of Christ in resurrection for nourishment to all the priests. Since we are the priests, we can enjoy Christ's love in His resurrection, the love in life. Of course, love is not a matter of power in ascension. Love is a matter of life in resurrection.

4. The Offerer's Portion

a. The Flesh of the Cattle—the Supply of Christ

The flesh of the cattle signifies the rich supply of Christ as our nourishment (7:15-18).

1) Of the Peace Offering
for Thanksgiving (of Emotion)
Good for Eating for One Day

The meat of the cattle of the peace offering for thanksgiving is good for only one day (v. 15). It can last only one day because the motive of this offering is shallow. It is presented out of the offerer's emotion, so it does not last very long. Our experience testifies of this. Sometimes we offer something to the Lord out of our emotions, but within a short time it disappears.

2) Of the Peace Offering for a Vow or a Voluntary Offering
(of the Will) Good for Eating for Two Days

The meat of the cattle of the peace offering for a vow or a voluntary offering (of the will) is good for eating for two days (vv. 16-18). The peace offering for thanksgiving is something emotional, whereas the one for a vow is something of the will and is stronger and deeper. We need to help the saints to realize that an emotional offering is good, but it does not last too long. We need to go deeper to present a voluntary offering. Because He is the Lord and we are His redeemed, we should do something in a voluntary way. There is no emotion involved here, but something strongly motivated from our will. This offering can last for two days because it is stronger.

b. Cakes of All Four Kinds as Described in 1), 2), 3), and 4), under 2a—Christ in His Humanity as Food to His Offerer

The four kinds of cakes which we have described earlier signify Christ in His humanity as food to His offerer (Lev. 7:12-13). They are the portion of enjoyment to the offerer. The more we offer, the more food we have.

5. The Congregation's Portion

The congregation's portion for their enjoyment is the flesh of the cattle, signifying the supply of Christ for nourishment, under the condition of cleanness (Lev. 7:19-21; 1 Cor. 5:8-11, 13b). The entire congregation enjoys the meat of the cattle, but they do not have a share of the cakes. The condition for the entire congregation to enjoy, to participate in, the peace offering is that they must be clean. First Corinthians 5 points out that today we are keeping the real Feast of Unleavened Bread. We need to keep this feast without any leaven, that is, without any sinful things. Whoever is living in sinful things should be cut off from the fellowship of the church, the Body. Such ones have no share in the enjoyment of the peace offering. This strongly indicates that today any saint who is still involved in sinful things cannot have the fellowship of the Lord's table. He has to be cut off from the fellowship of the Body.

THE CHURCH-BUILDING SERVICE

Scripture Reading: Eph. 4:16, 7, 12; 1 Pet. 4:10; Rom. 12:7a; 16:1; Acts 6:3; 1 Cor. 12:28b; Matt. 20:26-28; Col. 1:7; 4:12, 7; Eph. 6:21

OUTLINE

   I. The church being built by itself, not only through the joints of supply but also through each one part—Eph. 4:16.

  II. To each one of us grace having been given according to the measure of the gift of Christ for the building up of the Body of Christ—Eph. 4:7, 12.

 III. As every man has received a gift, even so minister the same to one another, as good stewards of the varied grace of God—1 Pet. 4:10.

 IV. The practical service—ministry—Rom. 12:7a; 1 Pet. 4:10:

    A. As deacons and deaconesses—1 Tim. 3:8-13; Phil. 1:1; Rom. 16:1.

    B. Serving others—Acts 6:3.

    C. Helping others—1 Cor. 12:28b.

    D. As a servant, even a slave—Matt. 20:26-27.

  V. The examples of such service:

    A. The Lord Jesus—Matt. 20:28.

    B. Epaphras—Col. 1:7; 4:12.

    C. Tychicus—Col. 4:7; Eph. 6:21.

In this lesson we want to see the church-building service, that is, the service which builds the church.

I. THE CHURCH BEING BUILT BY ITSELF,
NOT ONLY THROUGH THE JOINTS OF SUPPLY
BUT ALSO THROUGH EACH ONE PART

Ephesians 4:16 says, "Out from whom [Christ as the Head] all the Body, being joined together and being knit together through every joint of the rich supply and through the operation in the measure of each one part, causes the growth of the Body unto the building up of itself in love." This verse shows that the church is built up by itself, not by the Lord directly. The joints of supply refer to the particular gifted ones mentioned in verse 11: the apostles, prophets, evangelists, and shepherds and teachers. The Body builds itself up not only through the joints of supply but also through each one part, each member of the Body.

We have to stress this strongly. We are not in Catholicism or Protestantism. We are the church. In Catholicism there is the hierarchy of the pope, the cardinals, the archbishops, the bishops, and the priests. In Protestantism there is a hierarchy of pastors. But the church is an organism, the organic Body of Christ with all the living and functioning members. There is no hierarchy in the Body, the church.

We all have to endeavor to avoid any kind of hierarchy. It is so easy for the functioning ones and the non-functioning ones to fall into this snare. There is a natural tendency to have a hierarchy, just like there is a natural tendency for water to flow down from a mountaintop. This tendency still exists among us, so we must be careful to avoid it. Those among us who have the ability to function must be on the alert not to take others' opportunity to function. We must give the ground so that all the saints may have the opportunity to function, and we have to encourage all the saints, great and small, to function.

II. TO EACH ONE OF US GRACE HAVING BEEN GIVEN
ACCORDING TO THE MEASURE OF THE GIFT OF CHRIST
FOR THE BUILDING UP OF THE BODY OF CHRIST

Ephesians 4:7 says, "To each one of us grace was given

according to the measure of the gift of Christ." This grace was given to us for the building up of the Body of Christ (v. 12). Grace was given to each one of us without exception. We must convince the saints that there is no excuse for not functioning. As long as you believe in the Lord Jesus, you have been regenerated. In your regenerated spirit, there is a measure. We have to convince the saints of this and do our best to develop their measure.

III. AS EVERY MAN HAS RECEIVED A GIFT, EVEN SO MINISTER THE SAME TO ONE ANOTHER, AS GOOD STEWARDS OF THE VARIED GRACE OF GOD

First Peter 4:10 says, "Each one, as he has received a gift, ministering it among yourselves as good stewards of the varied grace of God." In this verse Peter points out that each one has received a gift. The Word says everyone has received a gift, so there is no excuse; we must minister this gift to one another. We have to serve one another with this gift. The word *minister* in Greek really means *serve*. A minister simply means a servant or a deacon. Everyone is a minister, a servant, a deacon, a steward, ministering grace to others. Since we all have received a gift, we need to minister this gift to one another as good stewards of the varied grace of God. This is the grace in many aspects. The varied and manifold grace of God can be fully ministered only when all are ministering, or serving.

IV. THE PRACTICAL SERVICE—MINISTRY

Now we want to see something concerning the practical service—ministry (Rom. 12:7a; 1 Pet. 4:10). When we refer to the practical service, we mean the practical ministry.

A. As Deacons and Deaconesses

The practical service, the practical ministry, in the church is by the deacons and deaconesses (1 Tim. 3:8-13; Phil. 1:1; Rom. 16:1). The deacons and deaconesses are the serving ones. First Timothy 3:8-13 gives us the qualifications of the deacons and deaconesses.

B. Serving Others

The practical ministry is one of serving others. Acts 6:3 says that seven deacons were appointed to take care of the practical need of serving tables. These ones were full of the Spirit and of wisdom.

C. Helping Others

First Corinthians 12:28b uses the term *helps*. This refers to the services of the deacons and deaconesses. These verses give us a clear view that the saints in the local church should take care of one another. If you need something, I should serve you. If I need something, you should serve me. The church life is not merely a matter of meeting. Serving one another should be a part of our communal life. In the early church life, the serving ones even took care of serving tables. Paul used the word *helps* in a very general way. This word covers everything. If a brother does not know where a barber shop is and you help him, this is the practical service and this is brotherly love. To help one another is the practice of the Body life in a communal way.

D. As a Servant, Even as a Slave

Our practical service should be as a servant, even as a slave. This is according to Matthew 20:26-27. The great ones among us should be slaves to others. At least we should be servants to serve others.

V. THE EXAMPLES OF SUCH SERVICE

In this lesson we want to give three examples of such service.

A. The Lord Jesus

The Lord Jesus said that He came not to be served but to serve, to minister (Matt. 20:28). He served us even by giving up His life. This shows that we even have to die for the brothers if there is the need. We have to lay down our lives for the brothers (1 John 3:16). The Lord Jesus is the example to us of serving the brothers even at the cost of our lives.

B. Epaphras

In the book of Colossians Paul mentioned Epaphras twice. Paul said that he was "a faithful minister of Christ" on behalf of the saints (1:7) and one who was always struggling on their behalf in his prayers (4:12). A faithful minister is a faithful servant. Epaphras went to Paul from Colossae, and came back from Paul to Colossae to serve the saints there. A minister of Christ is not only a servant of Christ, one who serves Christ, but a serving one who serves others with Christ by ministering Christ to them.

C. Tychicus

In Colossians 4:7 and Ephesians 6:21 Paul spoke of Tychicus as a beloved brother, faithful minister, and fellow slave in the Lord. These verses indicate to us that in the early days some of the brothers served the church full-time. Otherwise, they would not have been able to travel as extensively as they did. In ancient times to travel by boat from one place to another could have taken a few months. It took them a long time to go to a certain place and return, so surely they were serving the saints and the churches full-time.

We should point out that there was such a unique and special characteristic of the church life in the ancient days. The church life is not an organization in which people are hired and fired. The church life is a matter of love toward the Lord and toward the saints. Because some of the dear saints loved the Lord, loved the church, and loved the saints, they served others at the cost of their lives. In the early part of the nineteenth century, there was this kind of situation among the so-called Brethren. This is why they were considered as the fulfillment of the church in Philadelphia, the church of brotherly love. The service that builds up the church must be like this.

THE GRACE-MINISTERING SERVICE

Scripture Reading: Rom. 12:4-6a, 7a; Eph. 4:7; 1 Pet. 4:10; John 1:17b; 1 Cor. 15:10; 2 Cor. 12:9

OUTLINE

I. All the members of the Body of Christ being gifted—Rom. 12:6a.

II. Every member having been given grace—Eph. 4:7; Rom. 12:6b.

III. All the members being stewards of the varied grace of God—1 Pet. 4:10.

IV. The service in the church being the function of the members with grace.

V. Grace being God embodied in Christ as our enjoyment—John 1:17b; 1 Cor. 15:10.

VI. To serve in the church being to minister Christ as grace to others:
   A. First, we need to experience the grace of Christ in our own circumstances—2 Cor. 12:9.
   B. Then we minister grace to others through our service.

VII. The goal of our service:
   A. Not to accomplish things.
   B. But to infuse others with Christ as grace.

In this lesson we want to see the grace-ministering service. Romans 12:4-6a says that grace is given to every member and that every member has a gift. Ephesians 4:7 says that to each one of us grace was given according to the measure of the gift of Christ. Then 1 Peter 4:10 tells us that we have to be good stewards of the varied grace of God. John 1:17b shows us that grace is Christ Himself coming as the embodiment of God for our enjoyment. In 1 Corinthians 15:10 Paul said, "I labored more abundantly...yet not I but the grace of God which is with me." Then in 2 Corinthians 12:9 the Lord told Paul, "My grace is sufficient for you, for My power is perfected in weakness."

I. ALL THE MEMBERS OF THE BODY OF CHRIST BEING GIFTED

Romans 12:6a says that we all have gifts which differ according to the grace given to us. This shows that all the members of the Body of Christ are gifted. We have to impress the saints with this. They may know that all the members of the Body of Christ are gifted, but they do not use their gift.

II. EVERY MEMBER HAVING BEEN GIVEN GRACE

According to Ephesians 4:7 and Romans 12:6b every member has been given grace. We need to read these two verses to the saints repeatedly in order to impress them that all of them have been given grace. In this message what is needed is mainly to impress the saints. They may know some of these points, but they have never been impressed with them.

III. ALL THE MEMBERS BEING STEWARDS OF THE VARIED GRACE OF GOD

According to 1 Peter 4:10, all the members are the stewards of the varied or manifold grace of God. On this point we need much speaking. This is not a common thought to all the saints. God's grace is not only of one aspect; it has manifold aspects. The Pentecostals think that grace is just to speak in tongues. If you do not speak in tongues, you do not have grace. To those who are for healing, grace is a miracle. If you do not have miracles, you do not have grace. But the New Testament shows us that to serve the saints with a cup of cold water is also an aspect of grace. To clean the meeting hall and prepare the chairs for the saints to sit on is another aspect of grace. If a brother is very bothered by a certain situation, and I go to pray with him, that is still another aspect of grace. God's grace is manifold. We can illustrate this point to the saints in many ways.

The church is the best society and has the best communal life. In such a society with such a communal life, there is the need of many kinds of services. Every service is an aspect of grace ministered by the saints to one another. Thus, all the saints as members of the Body of Christ are stewards of the manifold grace of God. On the one hand, we are members of the Body of Christ, and on the other hand, we are stewards of God. Stewards are persons who have the commission to minister the rich supply to others. A steward is one who always supplies others with certain needs, so we have to help the saints realize that every brother and every sister today in the church life as a member of Christ should be a steward of God assigned by God, commissioned by God, charged by God, with some aspect of His grace to minister to others for their supply.

One brother, whom I knew for about thirty years and who is now with the Lord, is a good example of this grace-ministering service. He did not speak much in the meetings because he was not assigned with that kind of grace. But whenever I went to his locality in Taiwan, I always saw him serving in some way in the meeting hall. He was a retired general from the army who lived on his pension and spent all his time to serve the church. Even though he did not speak much in the meetings, the church received the greatest service from him. He was respected by all the saints and highly valued by the co-workers because of his service. He served the saints in many ways to meet their needs.

Of course, we expect that all of the brothers and sisters would function by opening their mouths to speak in the meetings. But we do not like to force the saints to do this, because some do not have the particular portion of grace to be speakers. If you ask certain ones to function, it is like putting them into a coffin. We should not do this. To some extent, we have to make this clear publicly. We can say that we realize that some of the saints do not have a speaking portion, so we would not force them to speak. They have an eating and a breathing mouth but not a speaking mouth. But they should still serve the church according to the grace which has been given to them. They can serve practically in something like vacuuming the meeting hall. All the saints will receive the benefit of their vacuuming. That is the "vacuuming" grace. We should illustrate the practical service to the saints in this way.

Some of the saints may be bothered about not speaking to such an extent that they dare not come to the meeting. They may not feel happy about coming to the meeting and may even feel somewhat shameful. They do not have that particular aspect of grace, so it is difficult for them to speak. But on the other hand, we have to make it clear that no one who has a mouth should take an excuse. You may be able to deceive people, but you cannot deceive the Lord. The Lord knows you are very talkative. A brother may not speak in the meetings so much, but he may speak a lot to his wife.

We need to dwell upon this point to impress all the saints that all of them are stewards entrusted with some aspect of God's grace. God's grace is manifold. You cannot say that you have never been given grace. You have been given grace. You do not have the aspect of grace that Paul had or the aspect of grace that some of the elders have, but you surely have an aspect of grace. God has given you something.

IV. THE SERVICE IN THE CHURCH BEING THE FUNCTION OF THE MEMBERS WITH GRACE

The practical service in the church, such as maintaining the meeting hall by arranging the chairs, cleaning the windows, mowing the lawn, and trimming the trees, is the function of the members with grace. While you mow the lawn, you may minister grace to others who are cutting the grass with you.

If we hired janitors to clean the hall, that would create

one kind of atmosphere. But if all the saints come to take care of this janitorial work in the meeting hall with much prayer, this makes a big difference. Then the hall becomes like the palanquin mentioned in the Song of Songs, built and prepared through the love of the virgins (3:9-10). The serving saints prepare the meeting hall to be the palanquin on which Christ can be carried. Such a meeting hall will surely be different from any kind of auditorium. When we enter into an auditorium, we have the sense of coldness. But when we come into our meeting hall, which has been prepared, vacuumed, and cleaned by so many virgins, the sense is different. We should not think that vacuuming the floor of the hall or cleaning even one window of the hall is a small thing.

In my hometown of Chefoo, one older brother was a manager of a big insurance company. He was wealthy, but every Saturday he came purposely just to clean five windows of the meeting hall. He told everybody to leave those five windows to him. Those five windows were the five "eyes" of the hall at the front. He kept those windows clean as crystal, and a number of saints were inspired and encouraged by his service.

The meeting hall of the church in Chefoo was greatly used by the Lord. One young man who was passing by the meeting hall on his bicycle read the verse which was posted on the outside of the hall. The verse was Acts 16:31: "Believe on the Lord Jesus, and you shall be saved, you and your household." He saw that verse, got off of his bicycle, and prayed and was saved by the Lord. After he came into the church life, he gave us this testimony.

One sister, who became a deaconess among us, was burdened to pray for the salvation of her husband, who was a good businessman in Shanghai. A brother among us was a friend of his, and he invited him to come to our gospel-preaching meeting on the second day of the new year. Because of his friendship with this brother and because of his wife, he felt that he could not reject this invitation. The night before he came to the meeting, he had a dream. In that dream he saw the meeting hall and a group of people at the entrance ushering people in. In his dream he entered into the meeting hall and walked up a stairway to the second floor. He saw his friend, who was a brother in the church, on the other stairway. He also saw the interior of the meeting hall. When he awoke the next morning, he was wondering about what he had dreamed. There was no need for his friend or his wife to urge him to go to the meeting, because he wanted to go to see if the hall matched what he had seen in his dream. When he went, he observed the meeting hall with the people outside the entrance ushering people in. He went inside the hall, and it was exactly according to what he had seen in his dream. He saw his friend come up the other stairway according to what he had dreamed. The hall was filled with people that day. After I preached the gospel in that meeting, he was the first one to stand up and pray to receive the Lord for his salvation.

My point in sharing this is that the hall in Chefoo was greatly used and blessed by the Lord because of the practical service poured out by so many saints. Every bit of that meeting hall was cleaned and prepared with much love and prayer. While the saints in Chefoo were cleaning the hall, they were praying. As someone cleaned a chair, he would pray, "Lord, I pray that whoever sits on this chair will be saved." They prayed definitely in this way.

In my whole life, I never saw a church life like the one in Chefoo. There were no great giants among us, but there was the service and functioning of all the small members. Even our children were looking for opportunities to serve the saints. While the gospel meetings were going on, some small rooms in the meeting hall were full of saints who were praying. They prayed until the meeting was over. That was a church fully in service. It was brought up and built up by every member functioning spontaneously. We have to let the saints know that the service of the church is the function of all the members with grace. This grace will reach people, nourish people, and even save people.

V. GRACE BEING GOD EMBODIED
IN CHRIST AS OUR ENJOYMENT

Grace is God embodied in Christ as our enjoyment (John

1:17b; 1 Cor. 15:10). Every member has to experience Christ as this grace. In whatever we do to serve in a practical way, grace is with us, and this grace will go out to reach others. This means we minister grace to others in our service.

VI. TO SERVE IN THE CHURCH BEING TO MINISTER CHRIST AS GRACE TO OTHERS

Regardless of what we do to serve practically, if we really do it in spirit, surely grace is with us. Then by our doing we will minister Christ as grace to others. First, we need to experience the grace of Christ in our own circumstances (2 Cor. 12:9). Then we minister grace to others through our service. Here we should stress that in order for us to experience Christ as grace, God always gives us certain kinds of circumstances. Sufferings and trials are often ordained by the Lord for us that we may experience Christ as grace. So when Paul asked the Lord three times to remove his thorn in the flesh, the Lord would not do it. He said that His grace was sufficient for Paul. Under certain God-ordained circumstances, we experience grace and accumulate grace to have a storage of grace in our Christian life. Then when we serve, we have something as grace to minister to others.

VII. THE GOAL OF OUR SERVICE

The goal of our service is not to accomplish things, even with something such as vacuuming the floor. Our goal is to infuse others with Christ as grace. We can infuse one another with grace while we are serving together. There should be no gossip, murmuring, criticism, or vain talk. Our talk should be our fellowship with grace to infuse one another. We need to have grace to minister to others. Actually, our goal is not to keep a clean hall, but to minister Christ as grace to others.

THE DANGER AND LOSS
OF NOT USING OUR GIFT

Scripture Reading: Matt. 24:48-51; 25:24-31

OUTLINE

I. The danger:
   A. Beating our fellow slaves—mistreating fellow believers—24:49a.
   B. Eating and drinking with the drunken—keeping company with people who are drunken with worldly things—24:49b.
   C. Hiding our gift in the earth—25:25:
      1. Being passive, not active, for the Lord's service.
      2. Merely keeping the Lord's gift, neither losing it nor gaining a profit by using it.
II. The loss:
   A. To be cut off from the Lord at His coming back—to be separated from the Lord in His coming glory—24:51:
      1. To be chastened dispensationally.
      2. In weeping and gnashing of teeth.
   B. To lose our gift—25:28-29.
   C. To be cast out into the darkness outside of the Lord's coming glory—25:30; 8:12.

In this lesson we want to see the danger and loss of not using our gift. The previous lesson tells us that we all have a gift. Now this lesson warns us that if we do not use our gift, this is dangerous, and this will be a loss. All these points are covered in detail in *Life-study of Matthew* (see messages sixty-three through sixty-six, pp. 733-774).

The greatest problem today with the Christians is that most of them do not use their gift. I would say that over ninety percent of the genuine Christians today neglect their gift. Of course, this is absolutely due to Catholicism and Protestantism. Because of these two big organizations with their hierarchy and clergy-laity system, most of the believers' gifts and functions have been annulled. They do not use their gifts, and they do not realize that this is a serious mistake which will cause a great loss to them. I feel we need such a lesson to warn all the saints among us and to stir up their heart to use their gifts.

We must stress the burden of the previous lesson to the saints once again. We need to see that all the members of the Body of Christ are gifted (Rom. 12:6a). In the Lord's parables in Matthew 24 and 25, the Lord indicates that every one of His believers has a gift. He did not give the ground for any of His believers to be excused from functioning. All believers are gifted persons.

Matthew 25 tells us that some have five talents, some have two talents, and others have one talent. At the very least, we are the one-talented ones. A saint cannot say that he has not received a talent. We have to strongly stress this one thing. We have to convince every saint among us that they cannot say that they do not have any gift and cannot do anything. This is a lie. According to the biblical truth, every believer has a gift. You may have the smallest gift, but you still have a gift. Everyone is talented; everyone is gifted.

Of course, Ephesians 4:11 speaks of the apostles, prophets, evangelists, and shepherds and teachers. The gifted persons mentioned here are those who have been endued with a special gift. But verse 7 says, "To each one of us grace was given according to the measure of the gift of Christ." *Each one* includes every member of the Body of Christ, each of whom has received a general gift. This shows that everyone is a gifted person and is responsible to use his gift. The Brethren did not like to use the title *elders,* so they used the term *responsible brethren.* This is a wrong term because every believer is responsible. Who is not a responsible brother or sister? We have to be careful not to use the term *responsible brothers,* because all of us are gifted and are responsible before the Lord to use our gifts for the building up of the Body of Christ.

I. THE DANGER:

A. Beating Our Fellow Slaves— Mistreating Fellow Believers

Matthew 24 speaks of the evil slave who "says in his heart, My master delays, and begins to beat his fellow slaves..." (vv. 48-49a). When we mistreat a fellow believer by criticizing, opposing, or despising him, that is to beat him in the eyes of the Lord. We have to say a strong word here. We can easily fall into this danger without any kind of realization. We can fall into criticizing the brothers and sisters. Sometimes we may oppose or despise some of the saints. Perhaps we would even fight against them. This is to beat the Lord's slaves, who are our fellow slaves.

B. Eating and Drinking with the Drunken— Keeping Company with People Who Are Drunken with Worldly Things

Matthew 24:49b says that this evil slave "eats and drinks with the drunken." The Lord's word in Matthew 24 is a parable. Since it is a parable, it must be interpreted. To eat and drink with the drunken is to keep company with worldly people, who are drunk with worldly things. They are drunk with their worldly enjoyment. This is the danger of not using our gift. Once we become a person who keeps company with worldly people, we would not be faithful to the Lord in using the gift He gives us, so we fall into danger.

C. Hiding Our Gift in the Earth

1. *Being Passive, Not Active,*
for the Lord's Service

In Matthew 25:25 the slothful slave said to his master, "I was afraid and went off and hid your talent in the earth; behold, you have what is yours." To be afraid is negative. We should, rather, be positive and aggressive in using the Lord's gift. To go off and hide the Lord's talent in the earth is too passive. We should be active in the Lord's work. If we hide our gift, we do not need to do anything. To be passive and not active for the Lord's service means we are hiding our gift and not using it.

2. *Merely Keeping the Lord's Gift,*
Neither Losing It nor Gaining a Profit by Using It

Merely to keep the Lord's gift and not lose it is not sufficient; we must gain a profit by using it. In this lesson we do not need to get into the full interpretation of this parable, because we can ask the saints to read some of the Life-study Messages in Matthew. But we must stress to them that actually to hide our gift in the earth is not to use it. *The earth* refers to the worldly things. As long as we do not use our gift, we are hiding it.

We have to point out these three dangers: mistreating fellow believers, keeping company with worldly people, and not using our gift to do the Lord's service. We have to point out that many are hiding their gift, not using their gift, because they do not serve.

II. THE LOSS:

A. To Be Cut Off from the Lord
at His Coming Back—
to Be Separated from the Lord
in His Coming Glory

When the Lord comes back, He will come in glory. In other words, He will be clothed in His glory. The unfaithful ones who did not use their gifts will be cut off from His glory at His coming back (Matt. 24:51). They will have no share in

His coming glory. For a full interpretation of this, we need to read the appropriate Life-study Messages on Matthew.

1. To Be Chastened Dispensationally

To be cut off from the coming glory of the Lord is a dispensational chastisement.

2. In Weeping and Gnashing of Teeth

The ones who are chastised will be in weeping and gnashing of teeth. Weeping indicates regret, and gnashing of teeth indicates self-blame. We do not know what this chastisement will be like, but we know that it will be a suffering.

B. To Lose Our Gift

Matthew 25:28 and 29 say, "Take away therefore the talent from him and give it to him who has the ten talents. For to every one who has, more shall be given, and he shall abound; but from him who does not have, even that which he has shall be taken away from him." These verses show that we can lose our gift because of our slothfulness. If we do not use our talent, the Lord will take it back from us when He comes back, and we will lose our gift. If we do not use our gift, this means that we waste it.

C. To Be Cast Out into the Darkness outside of the Lord's Coming Glory

The outer darkness is the darkness outside the Lord's coming glory in the manifestation of the kingdom of the heavens (Matt. 25:30; 8:12). To be cast out into the outer darkness is not to perish; it is to be dealt with dispensationally, to be disqualified from participating in the enjoyment of the kingdom during the millennium, for not having lived by Christ an overcoming life. In the millennium the overcoming believers will be with Christ in the bright glory of the kingdom (Col. 3:4), whereas the defeated believers will suffer discipline in outer darkness.

When we stress these points, some of the saints may be curious about what outer darkness is. We should simply tell them that we have never been there, so we really cannot say what is there; but we surely know that this is not a good place to be. This kind of darkness is not for the ones who will suffer eternal perdition. Those ones will spend eternity in the lake of fire. The outer darkness outside of the Lord's glory is neither the lake of fire nor the section of torment in Hades where all the perished sinners are (Luke 16:26, 23a, 28). It is a place of dispensational punishment for the defeated believers.

Some may say that this kind of teaching damages God's complete salvation. We should tell them that we have received the Lord's complete salvation and we believe in it. We also believe that if we are not faithful to the Lord today, He may chastise us. If the Lord chastises us in this age, this chastisement does not damage His complete salvation. Since this is the case, how could His chastisement in the next age damage His complete salvation? It is illogical to say this.

The Lord told us that when He returns, He will chastise His unfaithful servants (Luke 12:46-48). This is not our word. This is the Lord's word. We have to be faithful in teaching the Lord's word. We cannot cut off any verses. We have to present all the aspects of the Lord's word to the saints. It is wise to take heed to the Lord's warning (Luke 21:34-36). We need to impress the saints to take heed to the facts in the Bible.

Because we have been regenerated by the Lord, we are gifted. The Lord has given us at least one talent, at least one spiritual gift. If we do not use this gift faithfully, we cannot be in the place that the apostle Paul will be at the Lord's return. A saved person will not suffer eternally in the lake of fire. To say this is an insult to the Lord's redemption and salvation. But a saved believer may suffer some dispensational chastisement in outer darkness. He may be cut off from the Lord's presence in the manifestation of His kingdom. By that time the Lord's presence will be His glory. Thus, the defeated believers will have no share of the Lord's glory in the millennial kingdom.

This is not only scriptural but also logical. If we are living and walking in darkness today, how can we expect to participate in the Lord's bright glory in the next age? If we live in darkness today, we will be chastised in outer darkness in the next age. In this lesson we need to speak a practical word to the saints. We admit that we all have been saved and have received a gift from the Lord. But do we use His gift? Are we faithful? In this lesson we need to preach the gospel to the saved ones. This may help some of the brothers and sisters and stir them up to have a real hunger to serve the Lord. We all need to serve the Lord.

This word concerning the danger and loss of not using our gift is the word of our King. The Bible is not only composed of John 3:16 and Ephesians 2:8, which says that we are saved by grace. The Bible also includes Matthew 24 and 25, and we cannot neglect or put aside this portion. Fundamental Christianity shares the truth of John 3:16 and Ephesians 2:8, but they do not go on to share the truth revealed in Matthew 24 and 25. This is the teaching directly out of the mouth of the Lord Jesus. We cannot deny that we are slaves of the Lord, and each slave of the Lord has been given a talent. Now the problem is how we use this talent. We have to warn the saints that there is the danger and loss of not using our gift.

STRANGE FIRE

Scripture Reading: Lev. 10:1-11; 16:12

OUTLINE

I. The incense should be burned before the Lord with the fire from the altar of burnt offering—16:12.

II. The fire on the altar of burnt offering burns out all the natural and negative things before God.

III. The strange fire signifies the natural enthusiasm—10:1:

A. Not dealt with by the cross.

B. Not in resurrection.

IV. Strange fire in the priestly service causes death before God—10:2.

V. The priests should control their natural affection, not sympathizing with the victim condemned by God's holiness—10:3, 6.

VI. The offering of the strange fire might have been related to the drinking of wine—10:8-9:

A. Losing the discernment of holiness—10:10.

B. Being unable to teach God's people—10:11.

In this lesson we want to see the strange fire spoken of in Leviticus 10. All the serving ones need to know the significance of strange fire in the Lord's service. Nadab and Abihu, who were Aaron's sons and consecrated to minister as priests, offered strange fire which the Lord had not commanded, and fire came out from before Jehovah and consumed them (vv. 1-2).

I. THE INCENSE SHOULD BE BURNED
BEFORE THE LORD WITH THE FIRE
FROM THE ALTAR OF BURNT OFFERING

Leviticus 16:12 tells us that the incense should be burned before the Lord with the fire from the altar of burnt offering. It is by this fire that the two altars, the incense altar and the burnt offering altar, are linked together. The burnt offering altar was for the sacrifices. The incense altar was for the incense. But the fire linked these two altars together.

According to the Pentateuch, this fire that burned all the offerings on the brass altar came from the heavens (Lev. 9:24; cf. 1 Chron. 21:26; 2 Chron. 7:1). It was not a fire started by man; it was the fire that came from God. And that fire, from the time that it came, never ceased. The fire burned all the time, day after day, from evening until morning (Lev. 6:9). That fire was holy fire, not strange fire.

II. THE FIRE ON THE ALTAR OF BURNT OFFERING
BURNS OUT ALL THE NATURAL
AND NEGATIVE THINGS BEFORE GOD

The fire on the altar of burnt offering burns out all the natural and negative things before God. It burns everything into ashes. Anything that can ascend to God must first be burned at the altar with the divine fire. Whatever has been burned on the altar with the divine fire will be accepted by God. Thus, to burn the incense before God at the incense altar, the fire that comes down from God is needed. This divine fire, which burns out all the natural and negative things, is needed for our service.

III. THE STRANGE FIRE SIGNIFIES
THE NATURAL ENTHUSIASM

The strange fire signifies the natural enthusiasm (Lev. 10:1) not dealt with by the cross and not in resurrection. Here we have to stress and develop what it means for us to be dealt with by the cross in our enthusiasm so that we can serve the Lord. In order to be in resurrection, we have to pass through the dealing of the cross. We should not bring in our natural hotness. Whether it is good or bad, pure or impure, it is still natural.

IV. STRANGE FIRE IN THE PRIESTLY SERVICE
CAUSES DEATH BEFORE GOD

Strange fire in the priestly service causes death before God. Leviticus 10:1 and 2 say, "Now the sons of Aaron, Nadab and Abihu, each took his censer and put fire in it, and placed incense upon it, and offered strange fire before Jehovah, which He had not commanded them. And fire came out from before Jehovah and consumed them, and they died before Jehovah." Maybe the two sons of Aaron did this with a good heart, with a good intention, but still they were burned to death. The offering of strange fire caused death to these two priests before God.

We have to tell the saints that we are today's priests. As today's priests we must be careful about what we offer to God. We may have a good heart and a good intention in offering something to God, but if we offer the wrong thing, this can cause death to us. This does not seem like some serious sinful thing, but it is serious in the eyes of God. This death is mostly in the spiritual sense. Whenever we serve the Lord with a kind of natural enthusiasm, this brings in death to our spirit. This means we serve the Lord in a natural way. Any kind of natural service brings death to our spirit.

Many Christians today serve with a kind of natural hotness, a kind of natural enthusiasm. It is not something dealt with by the cross and altogether not in resurrection. In the past we have seen some capable ones who were hot in serving the Lord in the church. Gradually, the more they served, the more they brought in death to others and mainly death to themselves. They killed themselves in their spirit by their serving, so eventually they disappeared in the service. Their priesthood was lost. This is altogether the real significance of the death because of offering strange fire.

We must point out that we all need to serve, to function, and to use our one talent, our gift. But we must be careful not to serve in a natural way, with our natural hotness. Of course, the Lord does want us to be hot in the spirit, not cold or lukewarm. But we have to be hot in our spirit, not in our natural life. In Romans 12:11 Paul tells us to be "burning in spirit, serving the Lord." Any hotness in our natural life is strange fire to God, and this brings in death.

V. THE PRIESTS SHOULD CONTROL THEIR NATURAL AFFECTION, NOT SYMPATHIZING WITH THE VICTIM CONDEMNED BY GOD'S HOLINESS

After the death of the two sons of Aaron, Aaron was silent. He was told not to mourn for his two sons, who were condemned and killed by the holiness of God (Lev. 10:3, 6). This means that the priests should control their natural affection, not sympathizing with the victim condemned by God's holiness. It was difficult for Aaron as the father not to sympathize, so he needed to control his natural affection.

Thus, in our priestly service not only should the natural enthusiasm be rejected but also the natural affection should be controlled. Today everyone in the church life is a priest in the priesthood, and all the priests should control their natural affection, not sympathizing with anyone who is condemned or killed by the holiness of God. The fire on the burnt offering altar signifies God's holiness. It was God's holiness that burned on the altar day and night. Thus, the fire that came out to devour the two sons was the holiness of God.

In Leviticus 10 we can see two natural things: the natural hotness, the natural enthusiasm, and the natural affection, the natural sympathy. Both should be rejected. We should not bring in natural hotness, nor should we exercise our natural affection to sympathize with any natural ones.

VI. THE OFFERING OF THE STRANGE FIRE MIGHT HAVE BEEN RELATED TO THE DRINKING OF WINE

According to Leviticus 10, the offering of the strange fire might have been related to the drinking of wine. Right after Nadab and Abihu's death, God charged the priests not to drink wine. Verses 8 and 9 say, "And Jehovah spoke to Aaron, saying, Do not drink wine or strong drink, you or your sons with you, when you come into the tent of meeting, that you may not die; it is a perpetual statute throughout your generations." Every logical reader would consider that probably the two sons of Aaron offered strange fire to Jehovah because they were drunk. They drank too much wine.

Drinking wine, in the Bible, signifies the overenjoyment of the worldly, natural, or physical, material things. In other words, if we overly enjoy anything of this world, this always makes us drunk. When we are drunk, we are excited and out of control, doing things without regulation. It might have been that the two sons of Aaron were drunk, so they were excited and went beyond themselves to do something without being regulated. That means they offered strange fire in a presumptuous way. The offering of strange fire was a sin of presumption. They presumed to do something for God. Actually, that was not a real offering to God but something of their presumption against God's regulation.

People do presumptuous things because they have over-enjoyed something. They are drunk. When the priests are drunk, they lose the discernment of holiness (Lev. 10:10), and they are unable to teach God's people (v. 11). When we lose our discernment because we are drunk, we are not being regulated; so we surely cannot teach others so that they can be regulated.

The priests had a twofold function. One was to serve God; the other was to teach others. Today in the church our priestly function also comprises these two things: offering something to God to serve God, and teaching others. In offering things to God, we must have the discernment concerning what we should or should not offer. We need this clear discernment. Also, in order to teach others, we need our own learning by our experiences. If we are drunk and lose our discernment, we are unable to teach others, and we altogether lose our function of our priesthood. This is all included in the offering of strange fire to God. We need a clear vision of these things as a warning to us in our church service.

TAKING HEED HOW TO BUILD

Scripture Reading: 1 Cor. 3:10-15

OUTLINE

I. The unique foundation having been laid—vv. 10a, 11.

II. Building on the unique foundation—v. 10m.

III. Building with gold, silver, and precious stones—v. 12a:
- A. Gold symbolizing God's nature.
- B. Silver symbolizing Christ's redemptive work.
- C. Precious stones symbolizing the Spirit's transforming work.

IV. Building with wood, grass, and stubble—v. 12b:
- A. Wood signifying human nature.
- B. Grass signifying man in the flesh—Isa. 40:6-7.
- C. Stubble signifying lifelessness.

V. Every man's work will be tested by fire—vv. 13-15:
- A. If any man's work stands the fire, he will receive a reward.
- B. If any man's work is consumed, he will suffer loss:
  1. He himself will be saved.
  2. Yet so as through fire.

Following the previous lesson concerning strange fire, we need this lesson on taking heed how to build. These lessons may be considered as a pair, like two "sisters." They are brief, so they need much labor and development on our part.

I. THE UNIQUE FOUNDATION HAVING BEEN LAID

We have to tell the saints that all real service is a building work. The church service is not merely a work, but a building work. There are many works which are not building works. Only certain works are building works. Since we are going to serve, to build, we have to realize that we cannot lay a foundation. The unique foundation has been laid by the apostle Paul. Today we are still building on his foundation. Paul said, "According to the grace of God given to me, as a wise master builder I have laid a foundation..." (1 Cor. 3:10a). Then he said, "For another foundation no one is able to lay besides that which is laid, which is Jesus Christ" (v. 11).

II. BUILDING ON THE UNIQUE FOUNDATION

Our service must be a building work on the unique foundation (1 Cor. 3:10m). We cannot lay a foundation, nor can we build something on another foundation. We have to strongly stress these points. Even though all denominations claim that Christ is their foundation, actually many works in today's Christianity are building works on some other foundation. We do not like to set up social and charitable works such as schools and hospitals. The apostle Paul did not do this kind of work. Our service must be a direct building on the unique foundation. There is much charitable work in Christianity which is good, but it is not built upon Christ as the unique foundation. Whatever we do in the church must be something built directly on Christ. This is why the apostle Paul spoke such a strong word in 1 Corinthians.

III. BUILDING WITH GOLD, SILVER, AND PRECIOUS STONES

The proper building materials for the church are gold, silver, and precious stones (1 Cor. 3:12a). Gold symbolizes the divine nature of God the Father. Silver symbolizes Christ's redemptive work. Precious stones symbolize the Spirit's transforming work. This indicates that what we build upon the foundation of Christ should be something of the Triune God—the Father, the Son, and the Spirit.

IV. BUILDING WITH WOOD, GRASS, AND STUBBLE

We should not build the church with wood, grass, and stubble (1 Cor. 3:12b). Just as gold signifies God's nature, wood signifies the human nature. Grass signifies man in the flesh (Isa. 40:6-7). Stubble signifies lifelessness. Stubble is the stump of the crops after being reaped. With the stubble there is no seed, no life. We have to admit that most of the work in Christianity is according to and out of these three negative items—the human nature, the human flesh, and lifelessness.

I feel that this lesson is greatly needed among us. We may appreciate certain brothers' capabilities for doing things, but in the church life the main thing is not to accomplish things. The main thing is to build with the Triune God upon the foundation already laid, that is, upon the all-inclusive Christ. If we just depend upon our capability, talent, or skill to finish something, that means we are serving according to wood, grass, and stubble, not gold, silver, and precious stone. We need to serve with the Father's nature, in the Son's redeeming way with the cross, and by the transforming Spirit. If we serve according to ourselves, there is no transformation, no cross, and no divine nature. Then what we do is just a secular thing which has nothing to do with the church. The church is altogether a composition of gold, silver, and precious stone—the Father, the Son, and the Spirit.

V. EVERY MAN'S WORK WILL BE TESTED BY FIRE

The apostle Paul told us in 1 Corinthians 3 that every man's work will be tested by fire (vv. 13-15).

A. If Any Man's Work Stands the Fire, He Will Receive a Reward

Verse 14 says, "If anyone's work which he has built upon the foundation remains, he will receive a reward." This has nothing to do with salvation. In verses 14 and 15, both reward and salvation are mentioned. The reward is not for salvation. Neither can salvation replace the reward.

If our work, our service, is really of gold, silver, and precious stone, it can stand the test of fire. These materials will not be burned. If our work is with these materials, we will receive a reward. The reward in the coming age will be the richer and higher enjoyment of the Lord. Today in our church life, in our work, in our service, we enjoy the Lord. But in the coming age the reward will be the richer, higher, and greater enjoyment of Christ. Apparently speaking, that will be an entering into the manifestation of the kingdom of the heavens, but our entering the kingdom is for the greater, higher, and richer enjoyment of Christ.

B. If Any Man's Work Is Consumed, He Will Suffer Loss

Verse 15 says, "If anyone's work is consumed, he will suffer loss, but he himself will be saved, yet so as through fire." Wood, grass, and stubble are not good for building materials but good for being burned. Today many Christians are producing fuel for a burning to come. The more they do, the more they have something for burning.

If anyone's work is consumed, he will suffer loss. *Loss* here means that he will lose the reward. He will lose the richer, higher, and greater enjoyment of Christ. The Word says clearly, however, that he himself will be saved, yet he will be saved as through fire. This indicates some kind of punishment and discipline, not just a loss.

We saw in the previous lesson that we must avoid anything of strange fire in our service. Also, all the work of wood, grass, and stubble must be avoided. We must build with gold, silver, and precious stone.

THE IMPOTENCE OF OUR NATURAL BEING IN THE THINGS OF GOD

Scripture Reading: Eph. 2:1, 5a; 1 Cor. 2:14; Jer. 17:9; Eph. 4:17-18; Rom. 8:7-8; Matt. 16:24; Rom. 6:6; 7:24; Phil. 3:3

OUTLINE

I. Our spirit having been deadened—Eph. 2:1, 5a.

II. Our soul neither receiving the things of the Spirit of God nor being able to know them—1 Cor. 2:14.

III. Our heart being deceitful above all things and being incurable—Jer. 17:9.

IV. Our mind being filled with vanity and darkened in understanding—Eph. 4:17-18a.

V. Our will being hard—Eph. 4:18b.

VI. Our flesh being unable to be subject to God and to please God—Rom. 8:7-8.

VII. Our self needing to be denied—Matt. 16:24.

VIII. Our body being of sin and of death—Rom. 6:6; 7:24.

IX. Learning to have no trust in our natural being in the things of God—Phil. 3:3.

In this lesson we want to see the impotence of our natural being in the things of God. The impotence is the insufficiency. We may be very sufficient in other things, but we do not have any sufficiency, competence, or power in the things of God.

I. OUR SPIRIT HAVING BEEN DEADENED

The spirit of fallen mankind has been deadened (Eph. 2:1, 5a), so it is useless in the things of God.

II. OUR SOUL NEITHER RECEIVING THE THINGS OF THE SPIRIT OF GOD NOR BEING ABLE TO KNOW THEM

First Corinthians 2:14 says, "But a soulish man does not receive the things of the Spirit of God, for they are foolishness to him and he is not able to know them because they are discerned spiritually." This verse shows that our soul neither receives the things of the Spirit of God nor is it able to know them. A soulish man is a natural man, one who allows his soul (including the mind, the emotion, and the will) to dominate his entire being and who lives by his soul, ignoring his spirit, not using his spirit, and even behaving as if he did not have a spirit (Jude 19). Such a man does not receive the things of the Spirit of God, and he is not able to know them. Rather, he rejects them.

III. OUR HEART BEING DECEITFUL ABOVE ALL THINGS AND BEING INCURABLE

According to Jeremiah 17:9, our heart is deceitful above all things and incurable. The King James Version says the heart is "desperately wicked," but Darby's translation says it is "incurable." In the things of God, our heart is incurable; it is a hopeless case.

IV. OUR MIND BEING FILLED WITH VANITY AND DARKENED IN UNDERSTANDING

According to Ephesians 4:17-18a our mind is filled with vanity and darkened in understanding. Verse 17 speaks of the vanity of the mind and verse 18 of the darkened understanding. This shows that our natural mind is utterly useless in the things of God.

V. OUR WILL BEING HARD

Ephesians 4:18b speaks of the hardness of man's fallen heart. This indicates that the will, as a part of man's heart, is hard, stubborn. Thus, our heart is incurable, our mind is full of vanity with a darkened understanding, and our will is hard, stubborn.

VI. OUR FLESH BEING UNABLE
TO BE SUBJECT TO GOD AND TO PLEASE GOD

Romans 8:7 and 8 say, "Because the mind set on the flesh is enmity against God; for it is not subject to the law of God, for neither can it be. And those who are in the flesh cannot please God." Our flesh cannot do two things. It cannot be subject to God, and it cannot please God. We need to develop these points in our speaking to the saints. Both the Old Testament and the New Testament tell us that God hates the flesh. God wants nothing to do with the flesh.

In today's religion of Christianity, most of the service is either in the soul or in the flesh. This is why we have to see the impotence of our natural being for our service. We need to impress the saints that our flesh cannot be subject to God and cannot please God. Then the saints may ask, "What is it to be in the flesh?" We should tell them, "As long as you are not in the spirit, you are in the flesh."

The New Testament mostly gives us a contrast between the spirit and the flesh, not the spirit and the soul. Actually, not many people are soulish; most people are fleshly. Even the most so-called moral persons are fleshly. At God's creation man is called a soul (Gen. 2:7), but after the fall of man, man has become flesh (6:3). Thus, in Paul's writings concerning salvation and justification, he does not use the word *soul* but the word *flesh*. He says that out of the works of the law no flesh can be justified before God (Gal. 2:16; Rom. 3:20). The *flesh* here refers to man himself.

When the Bible says something about people in a positive sense, it uses the word *soul* as a term for man (Exo. 1:5). But when the Bible says something concerning man in a negative sense, it uses the word *flesh*. No flesh, no man, can be justified before God by the works of law. The flesh is the fallen man. If we are not in the spirit, surely we are in the flesh. We should not think that we are so good that if we are not in the spirit, we are in the soul, not in the flesh. Actually, today our soul is one with the flesh, which is the uttermost expression of the fallen tripartite man. So if we are not in the spirit, we are in the flesh, and our flesh is altogether impotent in the things of God. It is unable to be subject to God and to please God.

VII. OUR SELF NEEDING TO BE DENIED

Matthew 16:24 says that our self needs to be denied. This shows that the self has been condemned by God. God has condemned it, so we have to deny it.

VIII. OUR BODY BEING OF SIN AND OF DEATH

Our body is a body of sin and of death (Rom. 6:6; 7:24). It is very active in sinning because it is a body of sin, and it is altogether dead in doing the will of God to please God because it is a body of death. Sin in our body makes us very active to sin, and death in our body deadens us in doing God's will. Our fallen body can only sin. It cannot do anything to accomplish God's will or to please God.

IX. LEARNING TO HAVE NO TRUST IN OUR NATURAL BEING IN THE THINGS OF GOD

After reading the above eight points, we should realize that we cannot have any trust in our natural being in the things of God. In Philippians 3:3 Paul said, "For we are the circumcision, the ones who serve by the Spirit of God and boast in Christ Jesus and have no confidence in the flesh." To have no trust in our flesh is to have no trust in our natural being.

We have to learn to reject our natural being and exercise our spirit in everything. God's salvation makes our spirit the inner man (Eph. 3:16). This implies that our spirit is our new person as everything to us. Actually, we should not live another man; we should live only the inner man. Our spirit worships, prays, and should take the lead to do everything in our Christian life and service.

We should not exercise our spirit only when we come to the meeting. We need to exercise our spirit when we speak to our spouse and our children. We should purchase things by exercising our spirit. If we do not exercise our spirit, we are in the flesh. When we come to the meeting, we may act as one person, but at home and in our daily life we may be another person. This is wrong. We need to do everything by exercising our spirit. Otherwise our meeting is altogether theatrical, and our meeting hall becomes a theater. We do not want to be actors and actresses who merely talk about the things of God in the meeting hall. We want to be those who exercise our spirit, deny the self, and reject the flesh. We should not have a double personality, being one person in the meetings and another person outside the meetings. This is hypocrisy and is wrong. Our entire being must be strengthened into the inner man. We must live the inner man, that is, we must let our spirit do everything, and reject everything of our natural being.

Most of the time we remain in the realm of good and evil. We do good things not by the spirit but by our natural being. But God does not want us to remain in the realm, in the field, of good and evil by using our soul to do good and to reject evil. God wants us to deny our natural being and use our spirit. When we use only our spirit, we are out of the field, the realm, of good and evil. Then we are in the realm of life. When we are not using our mind, emotion, will, and fallen body, we are using our spirit. Then we touch only life. The spirit touches nothing except life.

First John reveals that our regenerated spirit, which is born of God, does not practice sin (3:9; John 3:6b), but this does not mean that we do not sin or are without sin (1 John 1:8—2:1). Some teach wrongly that a regenerated person does not sin and cannot sin. They teach the eradication of sin, saying that sin is altogether eradicated from a regenerated person. Of course, there is not such a thing.

Many years ago in Shanghai, there was a preacher who strongly taught the heresy of the eradication of sin. One day he and some of his followers went to a park which required them to purchase tickets in order to be admitted. He bought three or four tickets to be used by a total of five persons. Some of them entered the park with the tickets, and then one of them came out with the tickets and gave them to the others for them to enter. That preacher brought his young followers into that park in a sinful way. As a result of this, one of the young men began to doubt about the teaching of eradication. He went to the preacher and asked him if this was a sin. The preacher responded by saying that it was not a sin but a little weakness. But regardless of what term you use, sin is sin, and we are sinners. Although you may call it another name, it remains sin nonetheless. We should never accept a teaching which says that we have become so spiritual that it is impossible for us to sin.

However, even though we are still fallen, our regenerated spirit cannot practice sin. Fallen man has a spirit which is reserved for God Himself. To repent involves the conscience, and the conscience is a part of man's spirit (Rom. 9:1; cf. 8:16). For God's own purpose, He preserved a part of man for Himself, that is, man's spirit. Our spirit is precious. Only our regenerated spirit does not sin, so we have to live in our spirit.

KNOWING THE FLESH

Scripture Reading: Gen. 6:3a; Gal. 3:3; 5:17, 19-21; 1 Cor. 3:3-4; Gal. 4:29; Rom. 7:18a; 8:7-8; Phil. 3:3; Gal. 6:8a; 5:16, 24

OUTLINE

I. The fallen man becoming flesh—Gen. 6:3a.

II. The flesh versus the Spirit—Gal. 3:3.

III. The flesh lusting against the Spirit—Gal. 5:17.

IV. The works of the flesh that damage the church life—Gal. 5:19-21; 1 Cor. 3:3-4:

    A. Enmities, strife, jealousy, and outbursts of anger.

    B. Factions, divisions, sects, and envyings.

V. People of the flesh persecuting those of the Spirit—Gal. 4:29.

VI. Nothing good dwelling in the flesh—Rom. 7:18a.

VII. The flesh being enmity against God—Rom. 8:7a.

VIII. The flesh not being subject to the law of God—Rom. 8:7b.

IX. The flesh being unable to subject itself to the law of God—Rom. 8:7c.

X. The flesh being unable to please God—Rom. 8:8.

XI. Not trusting in the flesh—Phil. 3:3.

XII. Not sowing unto the flesh—Gal. 6:8a.

XIII. Not fulfilling the lust of the flesh—Gal. 5:16.

XIV. Crucifying the flesh—Gal. 5:24.

The subject of this lesson—"Knowing the Flesh"—is very simple. After the previous lesson on the impotence of our natural being, we need to see this. My burden in these few recent lessons is to help the saints in the Lord's recovery realize the real service which the Lord wants and to help them see that what Christianity does is absolutely condemned and repudiated in the eyes of God. This is because the works or services in Christianity are either by strange fire (natural enthusiasm), the soul, or the flesh. Now we need a lesson to help us know what the flesh is.

I. THE FALLEN MAN BECOMING FLESH

Genesis 6:3a is the first verse in the Bible which says something concerning the fallen man as flesh. This verse indicates that man fell to such an extent that he became totally flesh. The fallen man is flesh.

II. THE FLESH VERSUS THE SPIRIT

The flesh is versus the Spirit. In Galatians 3:3 Paul said, "Are you so foolish? Having begun by the Spirit, are you now being perfected by the flesh?" The flesh is condemned and repudiated throughout the entire book of Galatians (1:16; 2:16; 3:3; 4:23, 29; 5:13, 16-17, 19, 24; 6:8, 12-13), and from chapter three every chapter gives a contrast between the flesh and the Spirit (v. 3; 4:29; 5:16-17, 19, 22; 6:8).

III. THE FLESH LUSTING AGAINST THE SPIRIT

The flesh not only is versus the Spirit but also lusts against the Spirit. Galatians 5:17 says, "For the flesh lusts against the Spirit, and the Spirit against the flesh; for these oppose each other that you would not do the things that you desire." There is a warfare between the flesh and the Spirit.

IV. THE WORKS OF THE FLESH
THAT DAMAGE THE CHURCH LIFE

The apostle Paul spoke of the works of the flesh that damage the church life (Gal. 5:19-21; 1 Cor. 3:3-4). Here I do not list all the works of the flesh; I mention only the works of the flesh that damage the church life.

A. Enmities, Strife, Jealousy, and Outbursts of Anger

Enmities, strife, jealousy, and outbursts of anger are of one group, concerning evil moods and fleshly feelings.

B. Factions, Divisions, Sects, and Envyings

Factions, divisions, sects, and envyings are of another group, concerning parties. A faction develops into a division, and then a division becomes a sect. *Jealousy* and *envyings* are two different words in the Greek text. Jealousy is actually envy in a smaller state. When jealousy is intensified and becomes greater, reaching "manhood," it turns into envy. Envy is more bitter and more severe than jealousy. Paul classified jealousy with the first group of evil moods, but he classified envy with the second group of parties. This second group is not just a matter of evil moods but of evil doings. Envy begins with jealousy. When jealousy becomes mature, it is envy. The above two groups of items are the damaging items to the church life revealed in Paul's writings. First Corinthians 3:3 and 4 show that the flesh was a damaging factor to the church life at Corinth.

V. PEOPLE OF THE FLESH PERSECUTING THOSE OF THE SPIRIT

Galatians 4:29 says, "But just as at that time he who was born according to the flesh persecuted him who was born according to the Spirit, so also it is now." The children according to the flesh, like Ishmael, persecuted the children according to the Spirit, like Isaac. Paul said that now it is also the same. The people of the flesh always persecute those of the Spirit.

VI. NOTHING GOOD DWELLING IN THE FLESH

In Romans 7:18a Paul said, "For I know that in me, that is, in my flesh, nothing good dwells." We should not say that we have something good in our flesh. We may think that we have bad flesh and good flesh, but there is no such thing as "good flesh." Nothing good dwells in our flesh.

VII. THE FLESH BEING ENMITY AGAINST GOD

Romans 8:7a says that the mind set on the flesh is enmity against God. This is because the flesh itself is enmity against God. When the mind is set on the flesh, it also becomes enmity against God. We have to develop this point when we share it with the saints.

VIII. THE FLESH NOT BEING SUBJECT TO THE LAW OF GOD

Romans 8:7b says that the flesh is not subject to the law of God.

IX. THE FLESH BEING UNABLE TO SUBJECT ITSELF TO THE LAW OF GOD

Romans 8:7c goes on to say that the flesh is unable to subject itself to the law of God. Even if it wanted to be subject to the law, it would be unable to do so. Romans 8:7 is the strongest verse in the Bible describing the flesh. The flesh is enmity against God, the flesh is not subject to God's law, and the flesh is not able to subject itself to God's law. It does not have the ability. To expect the flesh to keep the law of God is like expecting a cat to fly. Paul was very strong to say that we should not expect that our flesh can keep the law or can subject itself to the law. It does not have the ability.

X. THE FLESH BEING UNABLE TO PLEASE GOD

Romans 8:8 says that those who are in the flesh cannot please God. Because the flesh cannot subject itself to the law of God, it cannot please God. It is impossible for the flesh to please God. All these points need much development for our sharing.

XI. NOT TRUSTING IN THE FLESH

In Philippians 3:3 Paul said, "For we are the circumcision, the ones who serve by the Spirit of God and boast in Christ Jesus and have no confidence in the flesh." The religious ones may worship and serve God while always boasting and having confidence in the flesh, but we should not be like this. We should not have any confidence in our flesh for our worship and service to God.

XII. NOT SOWING UNTO THE FLESH

Galatians 6:8a says that if we sow unto the flesh, we will reap corruption of the flesh. To sow unto one's own flesh is to sow for one's own flesh, with the desire and purpose of the flesh in view, to fulfill what the flesh covets. We should not carry out any kind of spiritual endeavor by our flesh. I may go to visit a saint in my flesh and not in my spirit. That is the sowing unto the flesh that will yield a harvest of corruption. Corruption will eventually come out of visiting the saints or the churches in this way. We should not invest in any spiritual things by our flesh or unto our flesh. If we do this, we will reap corruption of the flesh.

XIII. NOT FULFILLING THE LUST OF THE FLESH

Galatians 5:16 says, "Walk by the Spirit and you shall by no means fulfill the lust of the flesh." Walking by the Spirit keeps us from fulfilling the lust of the flesh.

XIV. CRUCIFYING THE FLESH

Galatians 5:24 says, "But they who are of Christ Jesus have crucified the flesh with its passions and its lusts." The flesh is good only for crucifixion. It must stay on the cross. In the church service, we must help all the saints to see that our motive and intention must be pure, without any element of the flesh. Ambition is of the flesh. No other work exposes our flesh as much as the church service. The secular work is absolutely according to the flesh, so this kind of work does not expose the flesh. But the church service is altogether a matter of the Spirit. Thus, whatever we do by our flesh is exposed.

In order to have the proper church service, every saint should know not only the Spirit but also the flesh. If we know the flesh and do nothing according to the flesh, there will be no jealousy, envy, or ambition among us. I feel that this lesson on the flesh is crucial. All the saints need to know this. The flesh is a terrible "gopher." Most of the time it is hidden, but sometimes it comes to the surface. A gopher is a good illustration of this. The flesh is a great undermining factor that damages the church life.

FURTHER KNOWLEDGE OF THE FLESH

Scripture Reading: Exo. 30:31-32; Gal. 5:26; 6:12; Matt. 20:20-27; Phil. 2:14; Matt. 12:36; Exo. 17:8-16; 1 Sam. 15:1-23

OUTLINE

I. The flesh having no share in the holy anointing oil—Exo. 30:31-32.

II. Things belonging to the flesh:
   A. Vainglory—Gal. 5:26.
   B. Outward show—Gal. 6:12.
   C. Ambition for leadership—Matt. 20:20-27.
   D. Self-confidence.
   E. Self-righteousness.
   F. Self-justification.
   G. Self-vindication.
   H. Self-exaltation.
   I. Being opinionated.
   J. Murmurings—Phil. 2:14.
   K. Reasonings—Phil. 2:14.
   L. Gossip—Matt. 12:36.
   M. Rivalry—Phil. 2:3.

III. The flesh fighting against God's people in their journey to attain to God's goal—Exo. 17:8-13.

IV. God being determined to blot out the flesh and to fight against it from generation to generation—Exo. 17:14-16.

V. God commanding us to utterly destroy the flesh—1 Sam. 15:1-3.

VI. We will lose the kingship by not utterly destroying the flesh—1 Sam. 15:4-23.

Now that we have had a lesson on knowing the flesh, we need a lesson on the further knowledge of the flesh. We need to know more about the flesh if we are to be those who serve the Lord according to His desire.

I. THE FLESH HAVING NO SHARE
IN THE HOLY ANOINTING OIL

In Exodus 30:31 and 32 the Lord charged Moses not to anoint any flesh with the holy anointing oil. The holy anointing oil, the compound ointment, signifies the consummated and compound Spirit. This indicates clearly that the compound Spirit is absolutely not for the flesh. When we are living and acting in the flesh, we are through with the compound Spirit, the all-inclusive, consummated, life-giving Spirit. Because the Spirit has nothing to do with our flesh, we have to be in our spirit. This is a serious matter. Eventually, the ultimate consummation of the Triune God is the consummated, all-inclusive, life-giving Spirit. If we are through with Him, we are through with God. Therefore, we must condemn the flesh to the uttermost because it has no share in the all-inclusive Spirit.

II. THINGS BELONGING TO THE FLESH

Now we want to see thirteen things belonging to the flesh.

A. Vainglory

In Galatians 5:26 Paul said, "Let us not become vainglorious, provoking one another, envying one another." Everything that is considered as a glory today, such as having a position or a name, is vain. It is vainglory. We should not seek for man's glory today. The real glory is the coming glory of God. Whatever is considered as a glory today is vainglory.

B. Outward Show

In Galatians 6:12 Paul spoke of those who desire to make a good show, an outward show, in the flesh. People like to make a show of whatever they are, whatever they have, and whatever they can do. Such an outward show belongs to the flesh. Whenever you like to make a show, you have to condemn it. To say this is easy, but in our natural being we make an outward show all the time. Whenever we want to make an outward show, that is fleshly. Of course, this has much to do with vainglory.

C. Ambition for Leadership

It is also absolutely fleshly to be ambitious for leadership (Matt. 20:20-27).

D. Self-confidence

It is very difficult not to have self-confidence. If we did not have self-confidence, our will might be weak. But we have to realize that self-confidence is fleshly.

E. Self-righteousness

When we use the term *self-righteousness,* we do not mean self-justice. Someone who is self-righteous always considers that he is right. We use *self-righteousness* in the sense of someone thinking he is never wrong, but always right.

F. Self-justification

Self-justification is another characteristic of the flesh.

G. Self-vindication

The desire to convince others that we are right, to vindicate ourselves, is also of the flesh.

H. Self-exaltation

Self-exaltation is another characteristic of the flesh. Thus, we can see that self-confidence, self-righteousness, self-justification, self-vindication, and self-exaltation are all aspects of the flesh. We should not forget that this is a lesson concerning service. We must help the saints to realize that in the church service, we have to condemn self-confidence, self-righteousness, self-justification, self-vindication, and self-exaltation. There should be nothing of the self in the church service. When we have these aspects of the self, we are absolutely fleshly, and the Spirit, the holy anointing oil, has nothing to do with us. If we are so self-confident, self-righteous, self-justifying, self-vindicating, and self-exalting, we lose the Spirit. The Spirit is gone in our experience.

I. Being Opinionated

Being opinionated is different from having an opinion. You may have an opinion and not be opinionated. An opinion is a concept. Everybody has opinions, but we should not be opinionated. To be opinionated is fleshly. The friction and the dissension among us come from our being opinionated. These things belonging to the flesh are the roots of the problems in the church service.

J. Murmurings

Philippians 2:14 charges us to do all things without murmurings, which are of the flesh. Murmurings are of our emotion and come mainly from the sisters.

K. Reasonings

Philippians 2:14 also charges us to do all things without reasonings. Reasonings come from the flesh. They are of our mind and come mainly from the brothers. We do not care for finding out the reason for things; we simply desire to live Christ. The four Gospels tell us a number of times that the disciples of the Lord Jesus were trying to find out the reason for certain things. But the Lord Jesus would not let them know the reason. The disciples would ask "why," but the Lord Jesus would not tell them why. If He had answered them, He would have been taking care of their reasonings. To take care of people's reasonings is to take care of the tree of the knowledge of good and evil. The Lord Jesus always took care of the tree of life. He did not care for people's reasonings.

Murmuring and reasoning both frustrate us from carrying out our salvation to the fullest extent and from experiencing and enjoying Christ to the uttermost. In the church service, we must learn to reject murmurings and reasonings.

L. Gossip

Gossip is another item of the flesh. It can be considered

as an unnecessary exchange of information. Gossip is idle talk with idle words. In Matthew 12:36 the Lord said, "I say to you that every idle word which men shall speak, they will render an account concerning it in the day of judgment." The Greek word for *idle* means "not working." An idle word is a non-working word, an inoperative word, a word that has no positive function and is useless, unprofitable, unfruitful, and barren.

M. Rivalry

Paul told us in Philippians 2:3 to do nothing by way of selfish ambition, or rivalry. Rivalry is different from competition. In a school, the students compete. In athletics, the athletes compete. Competition is not bad, but rivalry is evil. Rivalry is negative competition. Someone may give a good testimony, and another saint may want to give a better one. Someone may bring three persons into the recovery, and another may see this and want to bring in six. If you always want to be higher and better than others and have something more than others, this is rivalry. Rivalry is of the flesh.

If the saints in the church service, by the Lord's grace, exercise to avoid all the thirteen items of the flesh listed above, we will have a wonderful church service. It would even be good if some of these items could be on our wall as frameable quotes such as "No vainglory," "No outward show," "No ambition for leadership," etc.

III. THE FLESH FIGHTING AGAINST GOD'S PEOPLE IN THEIR JOURNEY TO ATTAIN TO GOD'S GOAL

Exodus 17:8-13 speaks of Amalek fighting against the children of Israel while they were journeying to attain to God's goal. Amalek signifies the flesh. This reveals that the flesh fights against God's people in their journey to attain to God's goal. As we follow the Lord on His way, the biggest subjective and inward frustration is our flesh. The flesh always frustrates, hinders, and fights against us in our journey. The church is delayed from going on mainly because of the flesh.

IV. GOD BEING DETERMINED TO BLOT OUT
THE FLESH AND TO FIGHT AGAINST IT
FROM GENERATION TO GENERATION

Exodus 17 tells us that the Lord swore to have war with Amalek from generation to generation (vv. 14-16). The children of Israel overcame Amalek through Moses and Joshua. Moses was praying on the mountain, while Joshua was fighting Amalek. Moses and Joshua are two aspects of Christ: the ascended Christ interceding and the indwelling Christ fighting. We have no other way to overcome the flesh except by the living Christ, who is the ascended One interceding for us and the indwelling One fighting within us.

This warfare cannot be settled once for all. It is a warfare that continues from generation to generation. Day after day and all day long, while we are still in the old creation, we have to fight against the flesh. God is determined to blot it out, but this is not easy. In the fight against Amalek, Moses built an altar and called the name of it Jehovah-nissi, which means "Jehovah my banner" (Exo. 17:15). This means that Jehovah is the banner for fighting. God is determined to blot out the flesh and to fight against it from generation to generation.

V. GOD COMMANDING US
TO UTTERLY DESTROY THE FLESH

In 1 Samuel 15:1-3 God charged King Saul to destroy Amalek utterly, and He told Saul that this was because of what happened in Exodus 17 when Amalek frustrated the journey of God's people to reach His goal. God commanded Saul to destroy everything belonging to Amalek, but Saul did not do it.

VI. WE WILL LOSE THE KINGSHIP
BY NOT UTTERLY DESTROYING THE FLESH

Saul lost his kingship because he did not utterly destroy Amalek (1 Sam. 15:4-23). This tells us that we also will lose the kingship if we do not utterly destroy our flesh.

In Galatians 5:19-21 fifteen items of the works of the flesh are listed. Fornication, uncleanness, lasciviousness, bouts of drunkenness, and carousings are related to the lust of the corrupted body. Enmities, strife, jealousy, outbursts of anger, factions, divisions, sects, and envyings are related to the fallen soul, which is very closely related to the corrupted body. Idolatry and sorcery are related to the deadened spirit. This proves that the three parts of our fallen being—body, soul, and spirit—are all involved with the corrupted, evil flesh. Thus, in order to deal with the flesh, we have to deal with the lustful body, the corrupted soul, and the deadened spirit. We need to deal with the flesh by the all-inclusive, life-giving Spirit.

THE DENIAL OF THE SELF

Scripture Reading: Matt. 16:23-26; Luke 9:25; Gal. 5:16b, 24; Rom. 7:18-21; Matt. 19:16, 20

OUTLINE

I. The difference between the self and the flesh:
   A. The flesh being the corrupted and transmuted body—Gal. 5:16b, 24.
   B. The self being the fallen and rebellious soul—Matt. 16:26; Luke 9:25.

II. When the flesh dominates the self, the self becomes an evil person—Rom. 7:18-21.

III. When the self subdues the flesh, the self becomes a "good" person—Matt. 19:16, 20.

IV. The self being independent of God—Matt. 16:23-24.

V. The self being the embodiment of the soulish life, one with Satan, and expressed through the mind—opinionated thoughts—Matt. 16:23-24.

VI. The self being the hidden, damaging factor of our service in the church.

VII. The self needing to be crossed out—Matt. 16:24-25.

In the foregoing lessons on service, beginning from lesson thirteen, we have dealt with many negative things that frustrate and damage our service. Lesson thirteen is on the danger and loss of not using our gift. Lesson fourteen is on the strange fire. Lesson fifteen shows us that we need to take heed how to build. We should not build with wood, grass, or stubble, but with gold, silver, and precious stones (1 Cor. 3:12). Lesson sixteen speaks of the impotence of our natural being in the things of God. Then we saw in lessons seventeen and eighteen that we need to know the flesh in a thorough way.

We have to help the saints realize that in the service of the church we must know all these negative things. If we are not clear about these negative things and do not have a thorough clearance from these negative things, we can never have a proper church service. If we are not cleared up from all these negative things, we are still in Christianity in nature. So it is worthwhile for us to stay with the saints on all these negative points.

In this lesson we want to see the need for the denial of the self in our service to the church. The outline for this lesson is simple, but there is the need for much development, labor, and prayer on our part to enter into its intrinsic significance.

I. THE DIFFERENCE BETWEEN THE SELF AND THE FLESH

There is a difference between the self and the flesh, but most Christians do not realize this or care for this.

A. The Flesh Being the Corrupted and Transmuted Body

At man's fall his body was corrupted, and then it was transmuted, changed. Galatians 5 speaks of the lusts of the flesh (v. 16b) and of the passions of the flesh (v. 24). The lusts and the passions are the evil things of our fallen body. The flesh is the corrupted and transmuted body. This is the most proper definition of the flesh.

B. The Self Being the Fallen and Rebellious Soul

The soul was created by God but it became fallen. When it became fallen, it became rebellious toward God. In Matthew 16:26 the Lord said, "What shall a man be profited if he gains the whole world, but forfeits his soul-life?" In Luke 9:24-25, *soul-life* is replaced with *himself,* indicating that our soul-life, our soul, is our self.

We have seen that God created a body for man, but He did not create the flesh. The body became the flesh by being corrupted. In the same way, the soul was created by God, but the self was not. The soul became the self by becoming fallen and rebellious. The source of the flesh is the body, and the source of the self is the soul.

II. WHEN THE FLESH DOMINATES THE SELF, THE SELF BECOMES AN EVIL PERSON

In Romans 7:18-21 Paul shows how the flesh dominates the self and how the self tries unsuccessfully to overcome the flesh. When the flesh, which is full of lusts and passions, dominates the self, the self becomes an evil person doing evil things.

III. WHEN THE SELF SUBDUES THE FLESH, THE SELF BECOMES A "GOOD" PERSON

Some people are very strong in their will or in their character, so to some extent, but not altogether, they can control their flesh with its passions and lusts. Matthew 19 speaks of a rich young man who considered that he was good in this way. He came to the Lord and asked Him what good thing he could do to inherit eternal life (v. 16). When the Lord told him to keep the commandments, he said that he had kept them (v. 20). No doubt, he was a "good" person. This shows us that when the self subdues the flesh, the self becomes a "good" person.

IV. THE SELF BEING INDEPENDENT OF GOD

The self is independent of God (Matt. 16:23-24). It does not care for God's will or for God's interest.

V. THE SELF BEING THE EMBODIMENT OF
THE SOULISH LIFE, ONE WITH SATAN, AND EXPRESSED
THROUGH THE MIND—OPINIONATED THOUGHTS

In this point there are three subpoints. First, the self is the embodiment of the soulish life. Second, it is one with Satan. Third, it is expressed through the mind, which is actually the opinionated thoughts (Matt. 16:23-24). We have seen already that the fallen soul is the source of the self, so the self is just the soul. The self is the embodiment of the soulish life.

At man's fall, Satan not only entered into man's body but also entered into man's soul. This is because Eve firstly accepted Satan's thought into her mind (Gen. 3:1-5). Then she ate of the fruit of the tree of the knowledge of good and evil, which entered into her body (v. 6). Before the fruit entered into her body, Satan's thought had already entered into her mind. Therefore, the fallen soul is one with Satan. This is also based upon what we see in Matthew 16, where the Lord rebuked Peter by calling him "Satan" (v. 23). At that time Peter was in the self, in his soulish life, so he became Satan. This proves that the self is one with Satan.

After addressing Peter as "Satan," the Lord said, "You are a stumbling block to Me, for you are not setting your mind on the things of God, but on the things of men." This shows that the self, which is one with Satan, is expressed through the mind as opinionated thoughts. Thus, Matthew 16:23-24 shows us that the self is the embodiment of the soulish life, is one with Satan, and is expressed through the mind, that is, the opinionated thoughts. The mind is the channel, the means, for the self to express itself.

VI. THE SELF BEING THE HIDDEN, DAMAGING FACTOR
OF OUR SERVICE IN THE CHURCH

We need to impress the saints that the self is the hidden, damaging factor of our service in the church. It is like a hidden worm, eating up the fruitfulness of our service. We may have very much service without any result of life because this worm, the self, is operating. If our eldership is not effective, no doubt, the self is there. If our ministry is not potent, the self is there. If our shepherding or fellowship with the saints does not work so well in life, we have to realize that the self is there. The self is the basic damaging factor, but it is hidden.

VII. THE SELF NEEDING TO BE CROSSED OUT

In Matthew 16:24 the Lord said, "If anyone wants to come after Me, let him deny himself and take up his cross and follow Me." The self needs to be crossed out. For dealing with the self, we need to bear the cross. This means that we must remain under the killing of the death of Christ for the terminating of our self. The self is so living, active, and aggressive, so we need to apply the cross every day and all day long.

If our self is crossed out, the ministry will be wonderful, the eldership will be wonderful, all the services will be wonderful, and there will be no problem, no dissension, and no division among us. The self is a great, hidden, damaging factor to our service in the church. We need to share this lesson with the saints with the ministry of life to give them a deep impression of our need to deny the self.

REJECTING THE NATURAL STRENGTH AND ABILITY

Scripture Reading: Exo. 2:11-15; Acts 7:22-30, 34-36; Heb. 11:28; Luke 22:31-34; John 13:36-38; 18:15-18, 25-27; Matt. 26:69-75; 1 Pet. 5:5-6

OUTLINE

I. The natural strength and ability having no divine element.

II. The natural strength and ability acting on their own, not according to God's will.

III. The natural strength and ability seeking their own glory and satisfying their own desire.

IV. The natural strength and ability needing to be dealt with by the cross.

V. The natural strength and ability becoming useful in resurrection for our service to the Lord.

VI. The case of Moses:
   A. Educated in all the wisdom of the Egyptians and being powerful in words and in works—Acts 7:22.
   B. Doing something for God's people according to his own will—Acts 7:23-26.
   C. Being put aside by God for forty years—Exo. 2:14-15; Acts 7:27-30.
   D. Learning to serve God according to His leading and to trust in Him—Acts 7:34-36; Heb. 11:28.

VII. The case of Peter:
   A. Being self-confident in his natural strength and ability—Luke 22:33.
   B. Being put into a test—John 18:15-18, 25-27.
   C. Becoming a complete failure—Matt. 26:69-75.

D. Learning to serve the brothers by faith in the Lord and with humility—Luke 22:32; 1 Pet. 5:5-6.

The most difficult and crucial thing concerning the Lord's service is to take care of these negative points which we have pointed out in these lessons. Anyone in the Lord's recovery who is not clear concerning all these negative points cannot render a proper service to the Lord. We may even be taking the lead, but if we are not clear about all of these negative factors, we cannot help the saints to do the church service in the profitable way of life. We may do a lot of things, and we may help the local saints to do a lot of things, but nothing may be profitable in life.

The service must be out of life and also unto life. In all the church service, every saint must be made clear about this. In the church service, we are not endeavoring to merely do things successfully. We are flowing life out to others. The service must be a ministry of life to others, a service unto life. It must be life flowing out of us as a life ministry to others. In order for this to happen, we surely have to take care of all these negative things, which are the obstacles, hindrances, and barriers to the flowing out of life in our service.

In this lesson we want to see that in the church service we must reject our natural strength and ability, which are acquired by us either through birth or through learning. Any of our natural strength and ability is unprofitable to the church service in life.

I. THE NATURAL STRENGTH AND ABILITY
HAVING NO DIVINE ELEMENT

Anything natural does not have the divine element in it, especially the natural strength and natural ability. To use our natural strength and ability is altogether against the basic principle of the church as the Body of Christ, because the church as the Body of Christ is altogether a composition of humanity mingled with divinity. The church as the new man must be full of the divine element. The Lord condemns Christianity because it has become a religion carried out by man's natural strength and man's natural ability. There is no development of the divine element there. But the genuine church is a composition of the divine element mingled with humanity. We must learn this as a basic lesson, and we also must impress every saint who partakes of the church service with this point.

In our service we must do everything in the principle of incarnation. The principle of incarnation is that the divine nature is wrought into humanity. When the Lord Jesus was on this earth, He did everything in His humanity full of the divine element. He did not do anything by the natural strength or the natural ability. He said that He could not do anything apart from the Father (John 5:19). The Father was within Him and one with Him in all His deeds, in all His words, and in all His works (14:10; 10:30). Whatever He did, whatever He said, and whatever He worked was altogether with the Father as the divine element. We need to consider whether the strength and ability we use for the Lord's service are natural or divine. We have to learn the lesson of rejecting our natural strength and ability, and we have to help all the saints to learn this lesson.

II. THE NATURAL STRENGTH AND ABILITY
ACTING ON THEIR OWN,
NOT ACCORDING TO GOD'S WILL

When both Moses and Peter were younger, they acted on their own, not according to God's will. Today it is possible that we may act and do some service for the Lord on our own according to our natural strength and ability, but not according to God's will. Because we have the strength and the ability, we feel we do not need to pray, to wait on the Lord, to seek the Lord's will, or to look for the Lord's leading. This was exactly what happened to Moses. When he slew an Egyptian to protect his fellow Hebrew, he did this on his own and not according to the Lord's will (Exo. 2:11-12). The sad situation in today's Christianity is that people work for the Lord mostly on their own by their natural strength and ability. They do not pray for the Lord's leading. They may pray only for the Lord to bestow His blessing upon what they do. They do not pray that much for the Lord's will, because they trust in their natural strength and ability.

III. THE NATURAL STRENGTH AND ABILITY
SEEKING THEIR OWN GLORY
AND SATISFYING THEIR OWN DESIRE

When we work in our natural strength and ability, the goal is to seek our own glory and the motive is to satisfy our own desire. If we see this vision, it will kill our self-seeking and impure motive. Actually, in the Lord's work, we should not have our own desire, and we should not have our own goal for our glory, for our boast. We should do things simply because the Lord leads us to do them. We should not do them because we have something to achieve for our goal. That is wrong. The goal must be the Lord's.

To kill our desire and our goal means to kill our strength and ability. Our own desire and our own goal for our glory are one with our natural strength and natural ability. The people of the world and even many Christians do things by their strength and ability for their desire and glory, but we have to condemn and reject this.

IV. THE NATURAL STRENGTH AND ABILITY
NEEDING TO BE DEALT WITH BY THE CROSS

The natural strength and ability need to be dealt with by the cross. To overcome and deal with sin is not as hard as this. To overcome our natural strength and ability is a great, subjective lesson; it is more subjective than dealing with sin. In a certain sense, our natural strength and ability equal our self, our natural constitution. Our natural strength and natural ability are the embodiment of our self. This is why after the denial of the self we need a lesson on rejecting the natural strength and ability and dealing with them by the cross.

V. THE NATURAL STRENGTH AND ABILITY
BECOMING USEFUL IN RESURRECTION
FOR OUR SERVICE TO THE LORD

The natural strength and ability are useful if they are dealt with by the cross. After being dealt with by the cross, they are in resurrection. Some brothers speak in their natural eloquence, but other brothers speak with an eloquence dealt with by the cross. This is the eloquence in resurrection. Some who are short of experience may ask what the difference is between the natural eloquence and the eloquence in resurrection. It is hard to explain, but if you have the experience, it is easy to discern. Only those with the experience can discern the difference between the undealt with, natural strength and ability and the strength and ability in resurrection through the dealing of the cross.

In resurrection something divine has been wrought into our strength and ability. Even some divine element has been wrought into our eloquence. When we speak, we need to have our eloquence dealt with by the cross. The cross always works the divine element into the person it deals with, bringing God into him. If you have never been dealt with by the cross in your eloquence, that is the natural eloquence with nothing divine. But if your eloquence has been dealt with, that kind of eloquence is in resurrection and is full of the divine element. In the natural eloquence, there is no God. But the "dealt with" eloquence in resurrection is full of God. After being dealt with, our strength and ability become useful in resurrection for our service to the Lord.

VI. THE CASE OF MOSES

We surely need to gain ability, but once we have the ability, we need to be dealt with. This was exactly what happened to Moses. The case of Moses is the best one to illustrate the matter of rejecting the natural strength and ability. No other person in the Bible is as good as Moses in this aspect.

A. Educated in All the Wisdom of the Egyptians and Being Powerful in Words and in Works

Acts 7:22 tells us that Moses was educated in all the wisdom of the Egyptians and was powerful in words and in works. He came out to work for God, to rescue God's people from the tyranny of Pharaoh.

B. Doing Something for God's People according to His Own Will

Moses did something for God's people according to his own

will (Acts 7:23-26). He was full of assurance that he could accomplish something, but he was carrying out his will, not God's will.

C. Being Put Aside by God for Forty Years

God purposely and sovereignly put Moses aside for forty years (Exo. 2:14-15; Acts 7:27-30).

D. Learning to Serve God according to His Leading and to Trust in Him

In those forty years Moses learned to serve God according to His leading and to trust in Him (Acts 7:34-36; Heb. 11:28). Moses eventually became a person who did nothing according to his will. He always acted according to the Lord's leading. The Lord led him, and he followed. He had no faith in his ability. Although he was very capable, he did not use his natural ability. His natural ability was dealt with, so it became an ability in resurrection. The ability in resurrection corresponds with God's move. If our ability is not dealt with, it is separate from God's move. But after being dealt with by the cross, our ability becomes one with God's move. Actually, God was wrought into Moses' ability. His ability eventually was full of God.

Exodus 2 shows us a natural Moses, a Moses with his natural strength and ability. That was purely, solely, wholly, and absolutely Moses without God. Then after chapter three we can see another kind of Moses, a Moses that was fully dealt with by God. After chapter three, God was in Moses and whatever Moses did in his acts and move was full of God, having the divine element.

VII. THE CASE OF PETER

A. Being Self-confident in His Natural Strength and Ability

Peter was self-confident in his natural strength and ability even to the point of thinking that he would follow the Lord both to prison and to death (Luke 22:33).

B. Being Put into a Test

Peter was tested and he denied the Lord three times, even before a little maid (John 18:15-18, 25-27).

C. Becoming a Complete Failure

Peter was absolutely defeated and became a complete failure (Matt. 26:69-75). He did have a heart to love the Lord, but he was too confident in his own strength, his natural strength. His love for the Lord was precious, but his natural strength had to be denied and dealt with. The Lord allowed Peter to fail utterly in denying the Lord to His face three times, so that his natural strength and self-confidence could be dealt with.

D. Learning to Serve the Brothers
by Faith in the Lord and with Humility

Through his failure, Peter learned to serve the brothers by faith in the Lord and with humility (Luke 22:32; 1 Pet. 5:5-6). Peter was really broken and was turned from the natural ability to something in resurrection.

We surely have to impress the brothers and sisters with this message. They all must learn this one lesson: to reject the natural strength and ability. Our natural strength and ability must be dealt with and put on the cross. Then they will be in resurrection and full of the divine element. Then whatever we do in the church service will be a ministry of the divine element to others. If our natural strength and ability are not dealt with, we will minister something natural to people by our church service.